The Development of Western Civilization

*Narrative Essays in the History of Our Tradition from
Its Origins in Ancient Israel and Greece to the Present*

Edited by Edward W. Fox

*Professor of Modern European History
Cornell University*

THE GREAT DISCOVERIES

and the First Colonial Empires

By CHARLES E. NOWELL

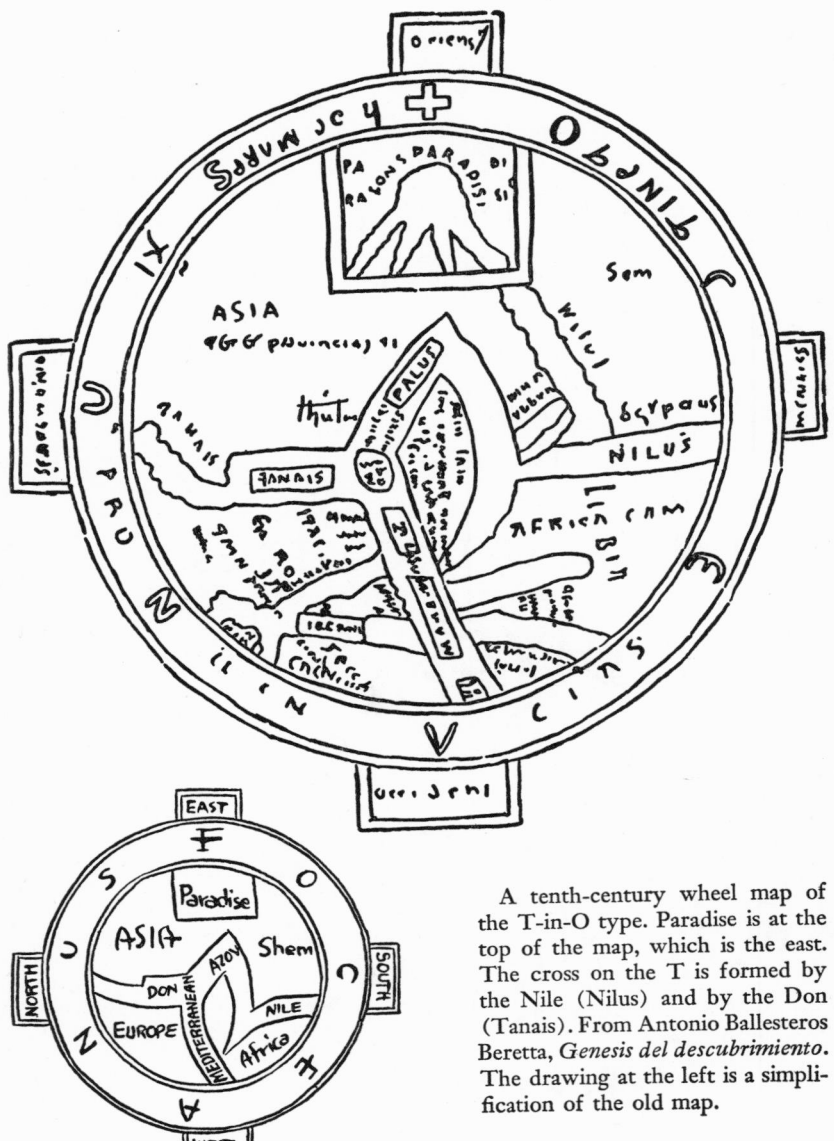

A tenth-century wheel map of the T-in-O type. Paradise is at the top of the map, which is the east. The cross on the T is formed by the Nile (Nilus) and by the Don (Tanais). From Antonio Ballesteros Beretta, *Genesis del descubrimiento*. The drawing at the left is a simplification of the old map.

THE

GREAT DISCOVERIES

and the First Colonial Empires

~~~~~~~~~~~~~~~~~~~~~~~~~~~~~~~~

CHARLES E. NOWELL

UNIVERSITY OF ILLINOIS

*

Cornell University Press

ITHACA AND LONDON

First published 1954 by Cornell University Press.
Published in the United Kingdom by Cornell University Press Ltd.,
2-4 Brook Street, London W1Y 1AA.

Second printing 1960
Third printing 1962
Fourth printing 1964
Fifth printing, with revisions, 1965
Sixth printing 1966
Seventh printing 1967
Eighth printing 1969
Ninth printing 1972

International Standard Book Number 0-8014-9848-1

PRINTED IN THE UNITED STATES OF AMERICA BY THE

VAIL-BALLOU PRESS, INC., BINGHAMTON, NEW YORK

Foreword

THE proposition that each generation must rewrite history is more widely quoted than practiced. In the field of college texts on western civilization, the conventional accounts have been revised, and sources and supplementary materials have been developed; but it is too long a time since the basic narrative has been rewritten to meet the rapidly changing needs of new college generations. In the mid-twentieth century such an account must be brief, well written, and based on unquestioned scholarship and must assume almost no previous historical knowledge on the part of the reader. It must provide a coherent analysis of the development of western civilization and its basic values. It must, in short, constitute a systematic introduction to the collective memory of that tradition which we are being asked to defend. This series of narrative essays has been undertaken in an effort to provide such a text for the introductory history survey course offered in the College of Arts and Sciences of Cornell University. It is being published in the present form in the belief that the requirements of this one course reflect a need that is coming to be widely recognized.

Now that the classic languages, the Bible, the great historical novels, even most non-American history, have dropped out of the normal college preparatory program, it is imperative that a text in the history of European civilization be fully self-explanatory. This means not only that it must begin at the beginning, with the origins of our civilization in ancient Israel and Greece, but that it must introduce every name or event that takes an integral place in the account and ruthlessly delete all others no matter how firmly imbedded in historical protocol. Only thus simplified and complete will the narrative present a sufficiently clear outline of those major trends and developments that have led from the beginning of our recorded time to the most pressing of our current problems. This simplification, however, need not involve intellectual dilution or evasion. On the contrary, it can effectively raise rather than lower the level of presentation. It is on this assumption that the present series has been based, and each contributor has been urged to write for a mature and literate audience. It is hoped, therefore, that the essays may also prove profitable and rewarding to readers outside the college classroom.

The plan of the first part of the series is to sketch, in related essays, the narrative of our history from its origins to the eve of the French Revolution; each is to be written by a recognized scholar and is designed to serve as the basic reading for one week in a semester course. The developments of the nineteenth and twentieth centuries will be covered in a succeeding series which will provide the same quantity of reading material for each week of the second semester. This scale of presentation has been adopted in the conviction that any understanding of the central problem of the preservation of the integrity and dignity of the individual human being depends first on an examination of the origins of our tradition in the politics and philosophy of the ancient Greeks and the religion of the ancient Hebrews and then on a relatively more detailed knowledge of its recent development within our industrial urban society.

The decision to devote equal space to twenty-five centuries and to a century and a half was based on analogy with the human memory. Those events most remote tend to be remembered in least detail but often with a sense of clarity and perspective that is absent in more recent and more crowded recollections. If the roots of our tradition must be identified, their relation to the present must be carefully developed. The nearer the narrative approaches contemporary times, the more difficult and complicated this becomes. Recent experience must be worked over more carefully and in more detail if it is to contribute effectively to an understanding of the contemporary world.

It may be objected that the series attempts too much. The attempt is being made, however, on the assumption that any historical development should be susceptible of meaningful treatment on any scale and in the realization that a very large proportion of today's college students do not have more time to invest in this part of their education. The practical alternative appears to lie between some attempt to create a new brief account of the history of our tradition and the abandonment of any serious effort to communicate the essence of that tradition to all but a handful of our students. It is the conviction of everyone contributing to this series that the second alternative must not be accepted by default.

In a series covering such a vast sweep of time, few scholars would find themselves thoroughly at home in the fields covered by more than one or two of the essays. This means, in practice, that almost every essay should be written by a different author. In spite of apparent drawbacks, this procedure promises real advantages. Each contributor will be in a position to set higher standards of accuracy and insight in an essay encompassing a major portion of the field of his life's work than could ordinarily be expected in surveys of some ten or twenty centuries. The inevitable discontinuity of style and interpretation could be modified by editorial co-ordination; but it was felt that some discontinuity was in itself desirable. No illusion is more easily acquired by the student in an elementary course, or is more prejudicial to the efficacy of such a course, than that a single smoothly articulated text represents the very substance of history itself. If the shift from author to author, week by week, raises difficulties for the beginning student, they are difficulties that will not so much impede his progress as contribute to his growth.

In this essay, *The Great Discoveries and the First Colonial Empires*, Mr. Charles E. Nowell recounts the story of one of the most colorful and fateful adventures upon which European civilization has embarked—the exploration of the entire globe. Not only did the effects of this adventure add powerfully to the acceleration of European development—which already was gathering momentum—but it decreed as the destiny of all human societies the necessity of exchanging the isolated independence in which they had grown for the ever-increasing intercommunication and interdependence which has gone so far toward fashioning the world in which we live today.

EDWARD WHITING FOX

Ithaca, New York
December, 1953

Contents

List of Maps

Introduction

ABOUT nineteen centuries ago Seneca, the Roman philosopher, wrote:

> Our descendants will one day know many things that are hidden from us, for some knowledge is reserved for future generations, when all memory of us will be gone. . . . The world would be small indeed if there existed no possibility of new discoveries. . . . A moment will come when all that has been concealed will surge to light as the result of time and prolonged study. There will be a time when our ignorance will startle our descendants, because all these things will appear perfectly clear to them.[1]

He seems almost to be addressing the explorers of a future era, urging them to press on into the unknown. They finally did so, somewhat later, perhaps, than Seneca had expected. The earth they discovered turned out to be very different from the earth that early imaginations had conceived.

The present story tells how one part of the human race— the western European part—investigated this planet. The great explorations lasted from the fifteenth to the seventeenth centuries and together they form an epoch called the

[1] *Naturalium Quaestionum* (author's translation).

Age of Discovery. Since then, of course, exploration has gone on, but its purpose has been to fill in the details of a geographical pattern whose broad outlines were already known.

Empire building inevitably followed in the wake of discovery. The Europeans explored with the aid of newly developed techniques and weapons which made them physically superior to the alien peoples they encountered. These aliens, in many cases, had to pay the penalty for their weakness by being conquered. Some of the empires built by the European pioneers have vanished by now; others survive at least in part.

If Seneca could have returned to earth thirteen centuries after his death, he would have learned very little about geography that was not already known in his day. But if he had waited fifteen or sixteen centuries for his reincarnation, he would have been truly amazed, for by then many of his mysteries were puzzles no longer.

CHAPTER I

The Background
of the Great Discoveries

THE Greeks developed science as we know it, and one of their oldest sciences was geography. They began, however, with a very small horizon. Their poet Homer (ninth century B.C.), who described the Trojan War and the wanderings of Ulysses, could scarcely think beyond the eastern Mediterranean and immediately bordering lands. He had some hazy impression of the Black Sea, since he knew the myth of Jason and the Argonauts who sailed through the Hellespont and Bosporus to seek the Golden Fleece. To him the earth was a saucer-shaped affair, inhabited on top. For Homer and men of his time, all land on earth was surrounded by Ocean, a stream forever languidly flowing around the rim of the disk.

As centuries passed, the Greeks gradually improved on this crude early concept. Both as traders and colonists they sailed the western Mediterranean and the Black Sea. Occasionally they entered the Atlantic, although the rising naval power of hostile Carthage in the west made such adventures extremely dangerous. The Carthaginians aimed at trade monopoly and had the unpleasant custom of drowning all Greek trespassers they captured.

Carthage herself might contribute to our story were her exploits better known. Unfortunately, the passion for monopoly made the Carthaginians keep their own discovery voyages the strictest secrets. All we know is that one of their citizens, Hanno (about 500 B.C.), sailed through the Strait of Gibraltar and explored a great distance down the African coast.

Greek Geography Develops

Greek geographical knowledge expanded in the fourth century B.C., when Pytheas of Marseilles coasted the British Isles and learned of northern lands beyond them. At almost the same time, Alexander the Great conquered the Persian Empire and pushed the Greek frontier of knowledge eastward to India and central Asia. It never advanced far beyond those regions, for although the classical world learned dimly of China, the easternmost conquests of Alexander were soon lost and Persia became for all practical purposes the limit of western knowledge of the Orient.

Meanwhile Greek philosophy took scientific forms and led to geographical speculation. The Ionian philosophers, who were Greeks living in Asia Minor in the sixth century B.C., knew that the earth was a body isolated in space. They did not consider it a sphere; they were more inclined to think it a cylinder with the inhabited part on top. Even so, the Ionian philosopher Thales was able to predict a solar eclipse from astronomical data. Hecataeus, a little later, earned the title "Father of Geography" by seeking geographical information far and wide and putting all the facts he gathered into a book.

The idea of a spherical earth seems to have originated at

about the same time with Greeks living in southern Italy. Perhaps Pythagoras was the first to grasp the truth; at any rate his pupils spread the belief. By the time of Plato (427–347 B.C.) it was generally accepted by learned Greeks, and Plato's disciple, Aristotle, who was the tutor of Alexander the Great, lived to incorporate the geography of his young protégé's conquests into his own learned works.

Following Alexander's conquests, a heavy Greek migration poured into the Near East, and this gave geographical studies a powerful stimulus. Alexandria in Egypt became the world's intellectual center and scholarship flourished there for centuries. Eratosthenes (third century B.C.) was one of the greatest Alexandrian scholars and one of the foremost Greek scientists. He estimated the circumference of the earth by measuring the angle of the sun's rays at Alexandria on the day of the summer solstice, having already learned that on the same day there was no angle at Syene (Assuan) to the south on the Tropic of Cancer. This gave him the arc of a circle, the length of which was the distance between Alexandria and Syene. To find the total circumference was then but a matter of simple arithmetic. Eratosthenes came close to the correct figure for the circumference, but missed it slightly because the Greeks of his day were a little off in reckoning the distance between Alexandria and Syene.

Roman Geography

The Romans built the greatest empire of ancient times, yet they showed no especial interest in exploration for its own sake. They conquered Britain and learned something of Ireland, besides having a faraway knowledge of Scandinavia and the Baltic. Their eastern conquests brought them in touch with the Red Sea and the Indian Ocean, and Greek subjects of the empire surely sailed down the east coast of Africa and beyond India and Ceylon. But these distant voyages can scarcely be called Roman achievements and they added little to the permanent store of information. There is no evidence that Rome seriously explored either the Atlantic to the west or the African Sahara to the south.

Ptolemy

Claudius Ptolemy (second century A.D.), an Alexandrian Greek living in Roman times, was the last of the famous ancient geographers. He is the one best remembered today, because his book of geography and world map have survived and because Europeans in the great discovery period had high regard for his opinions. His "Ptolemaic" system remained the one most in favor until it was superseded by that of Copernicus in the sixteenth century. Ptolemy believed the earth to be a sphere and also thought it the center of the universe, with moon, sun, planets, and stars revolving in orbits around it. His global knowledge extended from the Canary Islands in the west to the "Land of Silk," or China, in the east, though even here he made two fundamental errors. He underestimated the earth's size and exaggerated the eastward extent of Asia—miscalculations that exerted both good and bad influences upon explorers in the Age of Discovery.

The "Dark Ages"

When the Western Roman Empire fell to pieces in the fifth century, there came a general shrinkage of geographical knowledge. Wealth dried up and trade languished, as German barbarians divided and plundered the Roman provinces. Contact between Britain and civilization was for a time all but lost, and the Atlantic became again a neglected, if not a forgotten, ocean. In the seventh century the conquests of the Moslem Arabs threw an almost impenetrable barrier around the eastern and southern Mediterranean. As Christian Europeans now found travel in distant parts nearly impossible, fabulous belief and pious legend gradually gained sway over the western mind in all matters concerning the East.

Yet it would be wrong to say that geographical study—or at least geographical theorizing—ceased altogether. The so-called dark ages, from the fall of Rome to the Crusades, were never quite as dark as we mistakenly suppose. If knowledge declined, some people, even in the darkest centuries, believed that the earth is a sphere. Despite a persistent modern myth which dies hard, there was no religious objection to such a theory. To be sure, Cosmas Indicopleustes, a sailor who in later life became a monk, did fashion a theory of a flat earth. Moreover, he wrote vehemently on the subject, asserting that the spherical idea is not only blasphemous but ridiculous, since it involves believing that men can live upside down. Yet the vigorous way in which the good Cosmas attacked such wrongheaded notions proves that he was used to hearing them. Furthermore, he cannot be called a spokesman for the Church, which never made a pronouncement on the matter.

T-in-O Maps

The science of cartography or mapmaking, which the Greeks and Romans had developed, though not very highly, was one of those which almost died in the early Middle Ages. Men lacked the knowledge required for making accurate maps, so they drew theoretical or imaginary ones, perfectly aware that these gave no true picture of the earth. They reverted to Homer's old idea of a disk, not because they wanted to emphasize flatness but because they were trying to get all known lands on one surface. Jerusalem had to be at the exact center, for the book of Ezekiel (5:5) declares: "Thus saith the Lord God: This is Jerusalem! I have set it in the midst of the nations and countries that are round about her." The east, where the Garden of Eden was supposed to lie, must be at the top. Three almost shapeless land lumps, representing Asia, Africa, and Europe, surrounded a Mediterranean which a modern observer can recognize only with difficulty. Such drawings are often called T-in-O maps, because they give the earth an O shape, and their Mediterranean, bisected at right angles by perfectly straight Nile and Don Rivers, resembles a T. Moreover, with a symbolism dear to the mediaeval heart, the letters stood for *Orbis terrarum* (earth circle).

Norse Explorations

The only venturesome European explorers in the early Middle Ages were the Scandinavian Norsemen. Because of overpopulation, unpopular rulers at home, and sheer love of roving and fighting, large numbers of these hardy Norwegians, Swedes, and Danes left their native lands. Their formidable migrations poured forth in recurring waves from the eighth to the eleventh century. The wanderers traveled in fleets of small open ships, propelled by oars and driven during favorable winds by sails. The Norsemen frequently added to the hideous discomfort of a voyage by taking along their patient women, howling children, and seasick domestic animals. They thought nothing of keeping at sea for weeks, in every sort of weather. They had no compasses and steered by the stars and dead reckoning, yet they could set a true course and hold to it.

They explored and raided all lands within reach, and many of them settled in places that took their fancy. In the ninth century their extreme western wing commenced the colonization of Iceland. This island had a little earlier been discovered and slightly populated by Irish religious hermits. These, however, offered no resistance to the heathen Norsemen, who pre-empted Iceland and turned it into a republic which, with various ups and downs, has lasted to the present.

The next step was to Greenland. It is not certain just which Norseman discovered this huge, barren waste or precisely when he discovered it. Our knowledge begins with the fact that in 985 Erik the Red, a pagan Icelander who had been outlawed and exiled for manslaughter, organized a party to settle there. Erik, whose talent for real-estate promotion almost equaled his talent for homicide, hoped to attract many settlers to his new home. Inspired by the one patch of green grass in the whole wilderness, he named the country "green land," since, as he said, "people will be more likely to come here if we give the place a pleasant name." Under his leadership two settlements were made in Greenland, both west of Cape Farewell and hence both facing America. These colonies survived until their extinction, probably by starvation and Eskimo attacks, sometime in the fifteenth century.

Norse Discovery of America

By reaching Greenland, the Scandinavians had entered the New World; they immediately proceeded to discover mainland America. The actual discoverer was a ship captain named Bjarni Herjulfson, who in attempting to find the new Greenland colony from Iceland overshot his mark and encountered some part of North America. Against the wishes of his crew he turned away without exploring, and on reaching Greenland he incurred criticism for his want of enterprise.

About fifteen years later, Erik's Christian son Leif went from Greenland with one ship to explore the coasts sighted by Bjarni. He discovered three American lands, which he named Helluland (Baffin Island?), Markland (Labrador?), and Vinland (Newfoundland?). Leif and his crew were particularly impressed by Vinland, where they reported wild grapes growing abundantly. They also encountered a mild and pleasant climate, very much different from the harsh Greenland weather. Exactly what stretch of coast they explored is debatable; evidence points to Newfoundland, although we can scarcely be sure. The date of discovery is also uncertain but must have been soon after the year 1000.

Leif spent a winter in Vinland before returning to Greenland, and though he never voyaged there again, several other Norse parties visited the new land. On closer acquaintance it did not prove to be the enchanting place it had seemed at first. Leif had encountered no Indians, but the later visitors met savages whom they named Skraelings, or Screechers. The Skraelings were hostile and too numerous for the Norsemen, whose eleventh-century weapons gave them small advantage over American natives. Since Greenland itself was a remote and struggling colony, with no manpower to spare for dangerous adventures, the Norsemen seem to have lost interest. Perhaps Vinland voyages were given a bad name by Leif's sister Freydis, who appears to have resembled her violent father Erik. She went with the last-recorded expedition, and in Vinland she murdered five female shipmates, a performance which caused unfavorable talk in Greenland. There is, at any rate, no distinct account of voyages after Freydis returned from her bloody exploit in 1016, although there are some indications that Norsemen were later in both Vinland and Markland. We can at least be sure that they never wholly forgot these lands in the distant west.

The discovery of the Kensington Rune Stone in Minnesota, by a Swedish-American farmer in 1898, furnishes important evidence that in the fourteenth century another Scandinavian party entered North America through Hudson's Bay. Carved on this stone is a brief and moving description of the sufferings of a mixed band of Norwegians and Swedes, who were expecting early death at Indian hands. If the inscription is authentic, as now seems probable, it fits with other bits of evidence to show that the Norsemen had a longer and wider acquaintance with the New World than was once supposed.

Yet, while the Scandinavians were the first Europeans in America, their voyages were more interesting than important. Proof is altogether lacking that the later great European discoveries owed anything to the Norse exploration of Vinland. The Scandinavians failed to understand what they had found and failed to make any practical use of it. This is not to their discredit, for Europe was then in every way unready to colonize the world beyond the seas. Anyone with an ounce of curiosity would wish to know more about Leif and his adventurous crew; yet in every sense that counts, Columbus remains the discoverer of America.

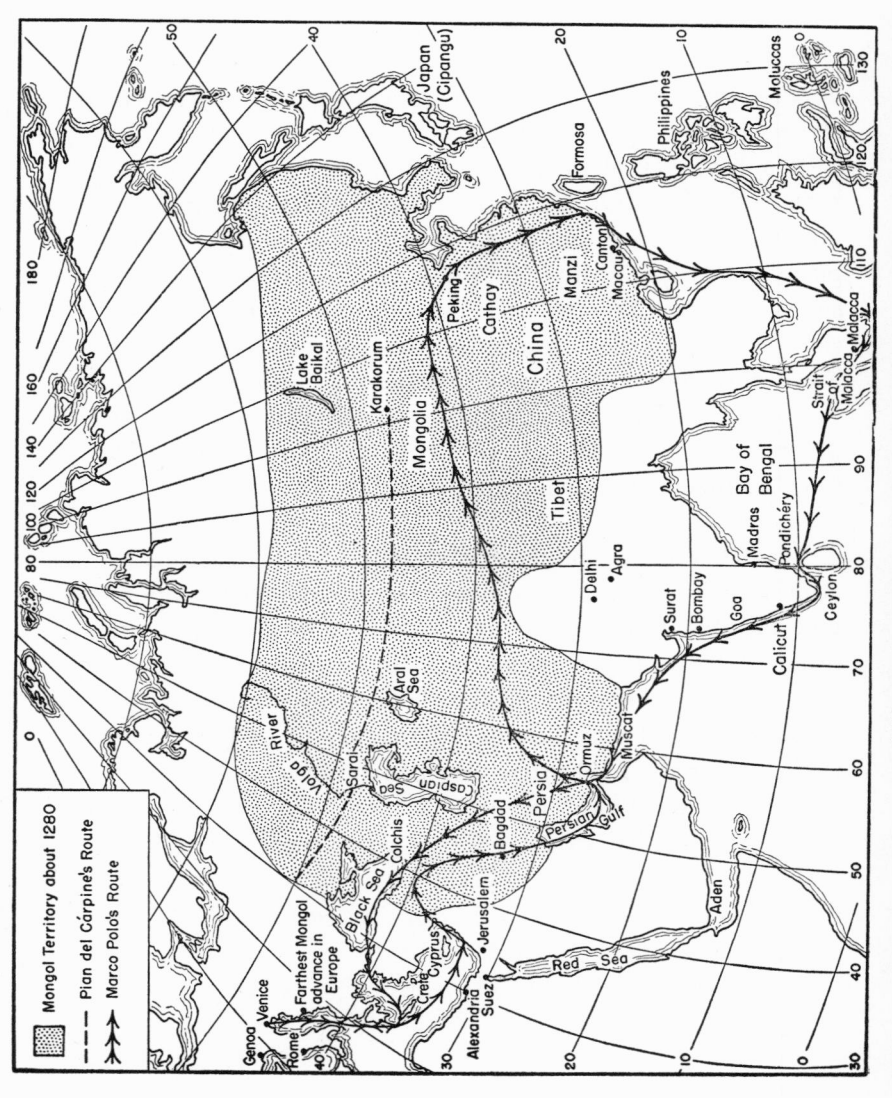

CHAPTER II

Europe Prepares
for the Great Discoveries

WHEN knowledge fails, man invariably substitutes his imagination. In the Middle Ages, Europeans had only a small store of geographical information, so to fill the huge gaps they drew on their well-stocked imaginations to create a picture of unknown places. Before the Crusades, they knew scarcely anything about the East beyond Palestine and Syria, yet the Orient held great appeal for them. Even during the Dark Ages, enough Asiatic spices, drugs, jewels, and fine cloth came westward in trade to encourage the belief that Farther Asia was a rich and wonderful place. Both literature and fanciful history lent colorful support to this opinion.

Legend and Romance

There was first the story of the Apostle Thomas. Soon after Christ's ascension, according to report, Thomas had preached the Gospel in India. The word India in the Middle Ages had no exact geographical meaning to Europeans; it was a convenient expression denoting the East beyond the Mohammedan world. Yet on the strength of the Thomas legend, it was supposed to be filled with Christians. Nestorian Christians did live in Asia; not actually in India, to be sure, but in lands to the north and west of it; and reports of their existence certainly filtered through to Europe. In view of the geographical darkness then prevailing, their exact location did not greatly matter to the western Christians.

Another source of misinformation about the East came from the Alexander romance. Mediaeval Europe had forgotten the real history of Alexander of Macedon, but everyone knew he had gone far into Asia as a conqueror. During the early Christian era, the entire episode had been distorted into legend by an anonymous writer with a vivid imagination. The Europeans, building on this basis, gradually transformed Alexander into a mediaeval hero, something like King Arthur and the paladins of Charlemagne. They wove into his story every element of wild fancy, and equaled *The Arabian Nights* in their descriptions of his Asiatic adventures.

Prester John

When the Crusades, after a fair start, showed signs of ending badly, Europe created the most powerful legend of all —that of Prester John. The Prester was supposed to be a mighty Christian ruler in Asia, living a pious and saintly life and possessing riches too great to count and armies too large to number. This wonderful sovereign, a descendant of the Wise Men who visited the infant Jesus, wished to communicate with western Christians and join them in destroying the unbelieving Moslems. A letter supposedly sent by Prester John began circulating through Europe in 1165. The writer, gathering up the whole stock and store of oriental wonder legends, poured it forth plentifully, extolling the

Prester's virtues and describing the size and marvels of his eastern kingdom. The papacy and western Christendom took it all quite seriously, and to this day no one knows who concocted the weird and wondrous document.

Europe believed in Prester John because it needed him. For centuries the West had fought a losing battle with its great antagonist, Islam. The first crusade had briefly turned the tide, but by the twelfth century Europe was on the retreat again. Nothing could be more welcome at this critical stage than news of an invincible ally in the enemy's rear, anxious to help grind the infidels to powder. Although as the years went by no signs of Prester John's promised aid were forthcoming, Europe refused to abandon hope and listened eagerly to any rumor that seemed to suggest the great eastern Christian sovereign.

Not until the thirteenth century were conditions sufficiently favorable in the East to permit Europeans to visit Asia in considerable numbers. Then they began traveling, some from religious motives and others for commercial reasons. Wherever they went, they kept an eye out for the cherished ally, Prester John. (Of course, Europe did not endow Prester John with personal immortality but thought of him rather as a member of a dynasty.) Occasionally candidates were found among insignificant Nestorian rulers, but these simply did not fill the bill; and the westerners concluded at last that no powerful Christian potentate existed in Asia. Early in the fourteenth century, Europeans moved Prester John to Africa and identified him with the Christian ruler of Abyssinia. There he remained, always an important factor in European speculations about unknown places and usually a main figure in projects of exploration. The undying belief in Prester John gave rise to a plan of European strategy to circumvent Islam and to secure a base in its rear. Prince Henry the Navigator had such a plan, and the idea figured somewhat in the thoughts of Christopher Columbus.

Mongol Empire

The European travelers whose reports removed Prester John from Asia were able to roam there because of a new and unprecedented circumstance, the rise of the mighty Mongol Empire in the thirteenth century. Genghis Khan (1167–1227), who began as the chief of an obscure tribe in northern Mongolia, intrigued and fought his way to the command of a military coalition of nomads dominating the caravan routes of east-central Asia. After subduing Manchuria and northern China, he turned westward and overran Turkestan and much of Persia. His armies, which for speed and discipline far outclassed any others of their time, cut a wide and bloody swath across central and western Asia, swallowing cities, provinces, and empires almost as fast as they could spur their hardy little Mongolian horses. During this early period of Mongol conquest, Europe heard distantly of the Khan and naturally identified him with the long-awaited Prester John. Could the grim old warrior have learned of this identification, it might have awakened in him the sense of humor he appeared so utterly to lack. Toward the end of his life, his armies made a brief raid into Russia, and from this Europe learned enough about the invaders to realize that they were neither Moslem nor Christian.

When Genghis died, the Mongols paused in their conquests a few years before raising his favorite son to the throne of the largest empire that history had thus far known. Their next western attack was launched against Russia, this time with the aim of permanent conquest. No people could stand against them, and after trampling Russia beneath their horses' hoofs, they burst into Poland, eastern Germany, and Hungary. Christian Europe, cowering in mortal terror at reports of the heathen invaders, finally met them in the flesh, but lacked both the unity and the military skill to offer much resistance. Poles, Germans, Magyars, and Czechs were routed, and the Mongols swept to the gates of Vienna and the shores of the Adriatic before turning back. Even then it was the death of the Great Khan (1241) and not Christian valor that stopped them in their course. When news came, borne by fast riders across Asia and Europe, that their mighty overlord had drunk himself into the grave, the Mongol leaders spurred for Karakorum, their capital north of the Gobi, where the new ruler was to be chosen. Western Europe still lay ripe for conquest, but its riches did not include the pasture land the Mongols prized so highly, and thereafter they apparently did not deem its conquest worth the effort. Russia became their European headquarters, and their later European raids were limited to Poland.

Missions to the Mongols

Christendom had a breathing spell, but for all anyone knew at the time it might be nothing more. Some European counteroffensive was clearly in order, although the pope sadly realized that Christian disunity made a crusade impossible. As a second best, the Holy Father sent a missionary delegation, headed by the elderly and corpulent Franciscan, Giovanni da Pian del Càrpine, to convert the Khan. Fra Giovanni entered the Mongol dominions in Russia and, somewhat to his surprise, was treated fairly well and even assisted on his journey. The Mongol deputy in charge of Russia deemed the Christian missionary important enough to be sent to the supreme lord of all the Mongols at Karakorum. There the Italian envoy was able to talk at least once with the new Great Khan, the grandson of Genghis. This lordly ruler snubbed the friar's proposal that the Mongols become Roman Catholics. Otherwise he seemed not altogether hostile to Europeans, and Giovanni was allowed to make his way homeward in 1248 to render his detailed report to the pope.

The truth was that the Mongols had only the crudest religion of their own, but they adopted a tolerant policy toward more advanced faiths. Indifferent themselves, they allowed Buddhism, Islam, and Christianity to be freely practiced in their empire. Moreover, they had instincts of good government. Though ruthless when conquering, they brought peace and comparative security to the subject lands. They wished to foster trade, not stifle it, and the vastness of their empire, stretching from the Pacific to Poland, gave splendid opportunities for commerce and safe travel. Though Fra Giovanni's mission failed, he could not have made the journey at all had no Mongol Empire existed.

Other Europeans followed Pian del Càrpine to the East. Several who wrote about their travels are known by name, and it is safe to say that many others undertook the adventure and remained anonymous. One important European visitor to Karakorum was Guillaume de Rubruk, a Belgian Franciscan who in 1253 was sent on a mission of conversion by the king of France. Friar Guillaume also failed in his proselytizing effort, although he had a diplomatic interview with another Great Khan, who was unfortunately too tipsy to make the audience an unqualified success. Nevertheless, Guillaume wrote a longer and somewhat better travel narrative than Fra Giovanni.

The Polos

Thus far the Europeans had not pushed as far as China. The distinction of arriving there first was reserved for the Venetian Polo brothers, Niccolo and Maffeo, who about 1265 reached the court of Kublai Khan (1260–1294). This famous ruler, another grandson of Genghis, had transferred the Mongol capital to Peking and was now concentrating on the conquest of southern China. Though the Polos were merely itinerant traders without official status, they returned to Europe bearing Kublai's request to the pope for Catholic missionaries to work in eastern Asia. The Khan's interest in western Christianity was probably no more than curiosity, but Europe remembered this flicker of attention for generations and wishfully took it to mean that the East was ripe for conversion to the Catholic faith.

On reaching home, the Polos found no pope on the throne of St. Peter, and after growing tired of waiting for the election of a new one, they returned to Asia without the missionaries but with the young son of Niccolo. This was Marco Polo, who left Venice in 1271 at the age of seventeen and returned in 1295 when he was over forty. The most important years of his life were thus spent in Asia, principally in China, where he acquired a grasp and understanding of the East that his father and uncle never gained. He became the historian of both Polo expeditions and the best interpreter of the Far East to mediaeval Europe. The *Book of Ser Marco Polo*, composed soon after his return to Europe, was a collaborative effort between Marco and a professional writer, Rustichello of Pisa. As a result of Italian city-state wars, these two found themselves for some months sharing the same cell in a Genoese prison. Rustichello proposed that they write the story of Marco's travels, and they worked together more to while away the time than to enlighten posterity. But when the book appeared it became very popular, at least with the general public; the learned preferred to believe what classical writers had said concerning the East. Meanwhile Marco was ransomed from prison and grew old and garrulous in Venice, boring his fellow citizens with endless tales of the wonderful lands and cities he had seen. After his death, many scholars were won over to believing what he had said about Cathay and Manzi (northern and southern China). His hearsay description of Cipangu (Japan), which he declared to be very rich in gold, appealed to some who thought that this island lay directly across the Atlantic from Europe.

The Polo journey to China was by no means the last in Mongol times. On a small scale, at least, the Church's missionary effort finally bore fruit, and from early in the fourteenth century there are reports of an archbishopric in Peking and a subordinate bishopric in southern China. It is difficult to know how seriously to take this, but the best guess must be that the number of converts remained small.

In 1368 a native dynasty drove the Mongols out of China and restored national independence. As a reaction to the conquest, Chinese policy became isolationist and antiforeign, but Europe did not learn of these changes for over a century. Even later than the time of Columbus, the West continued to think of a Great Khan as reigning in the East.

Changing Conditions

Shortly before the return of the Polos from China, the power balance in the Mediterranean tipped sharply, to the disadvantage of western Europe. The capture of Acre by the sultan of Egypt in 1291 eliminated the last Christian stronghold won during the Crusades. Sporadic efforts to drum up a new crusade failed, and Europe had to face a powerful Egypt standing athwart the best trade route to the East. The merchant republic of Venice made a quick adaptation to the new situation and concluded a commercial alliance with the Egyptians. Thereafter if Europe wanted oriental products it had to pay the prices of these profiteering partners.

By the opening of the fourteenth century, Europe had begun to look toward the Atlantic. Though the Crusades had failed, trading opportunities to the westward had improved. The emergence of Portugal as an independent kingdom and the growing economic importance of England and Flanders attracted the interest of the Italian trading cities. The great fairs of Champagne, where Flemish cloth could be exchanged for eastern spices, also lured the Italians. Presently they began sending trading galleys through the Strait of Gibraltar to the west European coast instead of using the earlier overland caravan routes.

Aids to Navigation

As sea voyages became longer, aids to navigation were needed and developed. Just who invented the compass—the Chinese, the Arabs, or the Europeans—is a matter of debate too long and involved to be settled here. Mediterranean seamen, chiefly Italian and Catalan, were certainly using a primitive compass before 1300. Although they knew nothing of the magnetic pole, they were already disturbed by the fact that their compass did not seem to point to the true north. The astrolabe, for finding latitude by astronomy, was also known in the thirteenth century. Unfortunately, the astrolabe could be used better on land than on the deck of a swaying ship, a factor that postponed its general adoption by mariners.

In the late thirteenth century, probably in the city of Genoa, there appeared the first portolan charts. The old T-in-O disks had illustrated a concept of geography that was mainly religious and could be of no possible use to navigators. A portolan, on the other hand, showed coastal contours in considerable detail and accurately gave distances from place to place. Its maker did not bother with inland points, nor did he exercise his imagination on coasts that had not been thoroughly explored. His business was to provide a working chart to help seamen reach the places for which they were bound. The earlier portolans were figured in terms of relative distance and not in latitudes, presumably because the navigator using them would not be likely to have an astrolabe. Later, during the fifteenth century, the portolans began to be constructed to a latitudinal scale.

At first these new maps showed only the Mediterranean coast, but as fast as the Atlantic shores became known in detail they too appeared. Next, the discovery or rediscovery of such island groups as the Canaries and the Madeiras caused them to appear on the portolans, in as accurate a position as the mapmaker's information would permit.

Early Discovery Voyages

Actual discovery voyages began. One of the bravest adventures ever recorded is the attempt by the Genoese brothers Ugolino and Vadino Vivaldo to sail to the "Indies" in 1291. Though evidence concerning the Vivaldi is scarce, it suggests that they planned to join some of their Genoese friends at the head of the Persian Gulf by going through the

Strait of Gibraltar. But how did the brothers plan to reach their goal—by rounding Africa or by sailing westward in the Atlantic? Since the Vivaldi kept the details of their plan a secret, we shall never know the answer, but whatever their intention, they failed. Their two light galleys were last sighted off the Moroccan coast; after that nothing is known of these brave Italians, who may well have anticipated the plan of another Genoese, Columbus, by a full two hundred years.

Other Italians with less grandiose plans continued to explore in the Atlantic. About 1312 a Genoese named Lanzarote Mallocello discovered the island of the Canary group that still bears the name Lanzarote and established a colony that lasted for several years. The Canaries had been known to a few ancient geographers such as Ptolemy and had even made a hazy appearance on mediaeval maps. But European contact with the islands, at least to our knowledge, had stopped during the Middle Ages.

Evidence from the portolans shows that the Madeira Islands had been rediscovered before the year 1330, and by 1351 an island group resembling the Azores had begun to appear on the charts. But we cannot be sure these were the real Azores. They may have been merely a cluster of imaginary islands, since European cartographers, even the makers of portolans, used a great deal of imagination when dealing with the unknown Atlantic. Maps of the fourteenth and fifteenth century dotted the ocean with fantastic islands bearing such labels as Mayda, Antilia, St. Brandan's Isle, and Brazil!

Not all the early exploration was the work of Italians. The Catalans and Majorcans were also able mariners and showed an interest in exploring the mainland coast of Africa. One of their voyagers, Jacme Ferrer, departed in 1346 to search for a "river of gold." Gold had long moved by caravan across the Sahara from Timbuktu to Europe; the Catalans evidently thought they could reach the gold country by sailing up a large river, probably the Senegal, which was reported to flow westward from central Africa to the Atlantic. Jacme Ferrer apparently died in this attempt, for surely his return from the Senegal, with or without gold, would have created excitement enough in Catalonia to provoke written comment and perhaps lead to further expeditions.

Thus between 1290 and 1350 a start was made toward exploring the Atlantic. But interest soon subsided and during the next fifty years some of the little knowledge already gained was lost. Genoese and Catalans had thus far led in discovery, but these were Mediterranean peoples, operating far from their bases and from their countries' main interests. Further improvements in navigation were needed before the Europeans could make long voyages. The Genoese and Catalan ships were mostly galleys with only a limited range on the ocean. They depended on rowers, whose large numbers and need for space made it difficult either to carry food for a long voyage or to bear substantial cargo. Sailing vessels, such as were gradually being developed, had several advantages: they could cope better with Atlantic winds, they had more cargo space, and they eliminated the need for the unwieldy gangs of rowers who propelled the galleys.

Valuable as their preliminary work was, the future of exploration did not belong to the Genoese and Catalans. It was Portugal and Castile, both facing the Atlantic, that ultimately developed efficient ocean-going ships and became the pioneers in distant adventure and great discovery.

CHAPTER III

Portugal and the East

THE modern world owes to Portugal the first planned and organized program of geographical discovery. That little nation became independent in the twelfth century, as a by-product of the Christian crusade to recover the Iberian peninsula from the Moors. Afonso Henriques, who began as Count of Portugal, shook loose from his Castilian overlord and took the title of king in 1140. He then drove southward, conquering or expelling the Moslems as he advanced, and his successors continued the work until by 1249 the liberation had been completed. Portugal in Europe had attained its present size. Over a hundred years later the small kingdom had to stand off the might of powerful Castile, which was intent on reannexing it, but the patriotic Portuguese proved equal to the challenge. Rallying behind their new and popular sovereign, of the house of Avís, they defeated the Castilians in 1385 and insured Portuguese independence for the next two centuries.

By this time there were already strong signs that Portugal's future lay on the ocean. Geographically the country was a narrow coastal strip without much hinterland. Trade by sea existed, some of it already borne in Portuguese ships. The people were hardy and warlike, anxious to carry the fight

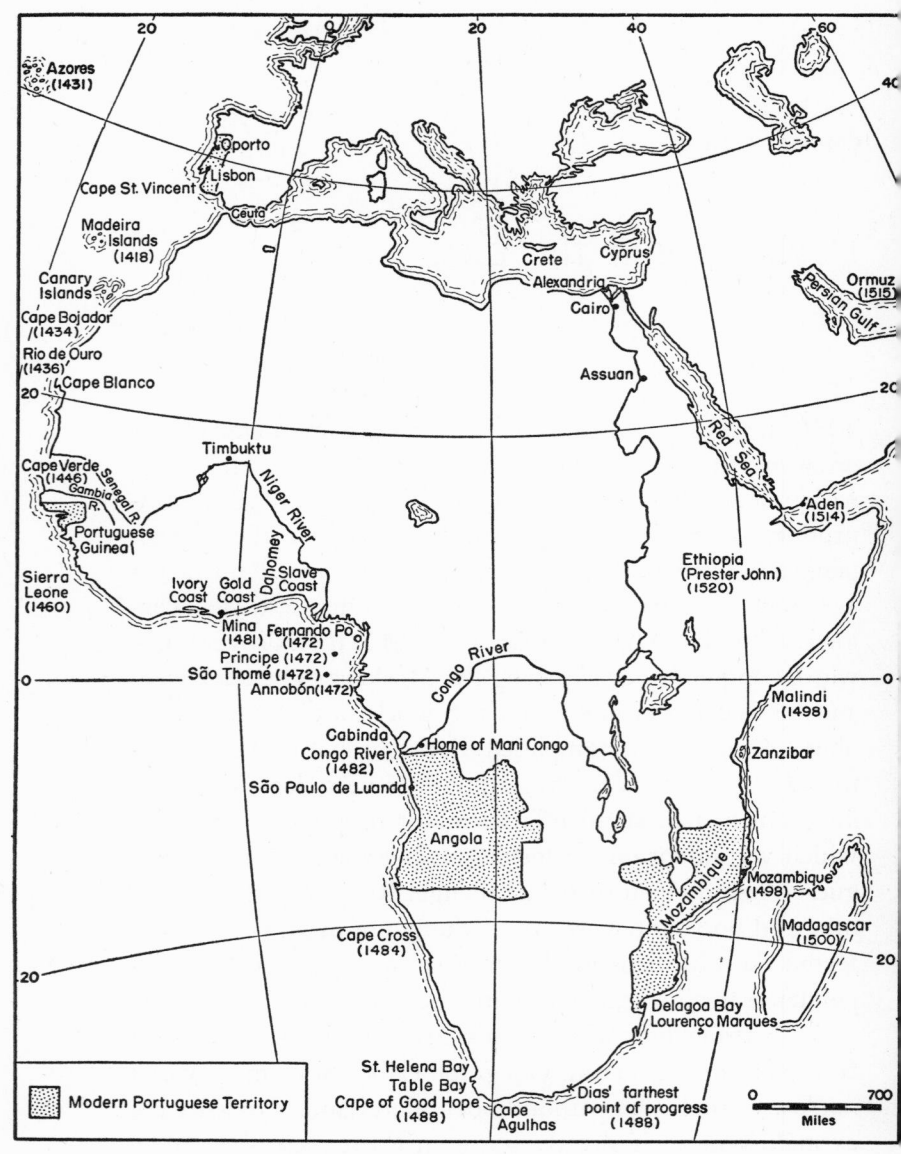

Africa and fifteenth-century Portuguese discoveries.

against the Moslems into Africa. Although the kingdom was small, it was by 1400 more compact and unified than were the larger European states. And for the particular direction in which sea exploration was to go, Portugal possessed the best point of departure on the European Continent.

Henry the Navigator

King John I (1385–1433), the founder of the Avís dynasty, had a gifted group of sons of whom the famous Prince Henry was the third. This prince and his brothers persuaded their father to lead a fleet and army across the strait in 1415 to capture the Moroccan seaport of Ceuta. Though the old king undertook this adventure with no thought beyond the immediate military advantage involved, Henry, who accompanied his father, looked upon Ceuta as a mere beginning. He studied Africa: its people, its trade routes, and its known resources. He became especially interested in the reports of gold from the distant south. He also wished to know how far the Islamic religion extended and what peoples lay beyond. Could they possibly be Christians? By this time the ruler of Abyssinia was positively identified with Prester John, but who knew how much of Africa the Prester's kingdom covered? When Henry heard reports of a great empire in the Sahara, he leaped to the conclusion that this was the domain of Prester John. The Saharan empire, though it had existed a few years earlier, had already broken up and of course had nothing to do with Abyssinia, which lay two thousand miles farther east.

With Henry the search for gold probably came first, for Portugal then suffered from a severe shortage of that precious metal and badly needed a new source of supply. So, for that matter, did all western Europe. The Egyptian-

Venetian monopoly of the Asiatic spice trade through the Red Sea and Alexandria had set up an adverse trade balance that was bleeding the West of its currency.

Whether Henry was also a religious crusader is hard to tell. Although in youth he had his gayer moments, he was pious in maturer years and lived a monkish life. He unquestionably wished to convert all Africans found in the course of exploration, and he had a great desire to make contact with Prester John. But all through his career—even though he freely used the resources of the Portuguese Order of Christ, of which he was grand master—he seemed mainly concerned with profit, perhaps because his work was expensive and he needed revenue to carry it on.

Since the prince never sailed with his voyagers, his surname "Navigator" is not exactly appropriate, but he was nevertheless the heart and soul of the exploring effort. He did the planning and financing and supervised the collating of data. He set up headquarters at the peninsula of Sagres, at the southwestern corner of Portugal, where he assembled a galaxy of talented seamen and scientists. Foreigners who wished to help were as welcome as Portuguese; Henry's servants included Italians, Catalans, and even a Dane.

His first important achievements were the discovery and colonization of the Madeiras and of the Azores. The prince probably knew that these were actually rediscoveries, and in all likelihood he used older maps of Italian and Catalan origin in directing his captains to the islands. Neither group had inhabitants, for although sighted in the previous century by Italians, they had never been occupied. Henry now sent colonists as fast as possible. The settlers from Portugal were placed under proprietors called donataries, who held their land grants on feudal terms. The islands showed a profit almost from the start. Madeira became an exporter of sugar and wine, while the Azores bred excellent livestock. Henry also made a gesture toward the Canary Islands, which were populated by a magnificent breed of warlike white savages. But Castile had begun the conquest of the Canaries in 1402, and Henry decided to avoid international complications by concentrating his efforts elsewhere.

The Coast of Africa

Cape Bojador, in southern Morocco, stood in the way of exploration to the south. Tradition said this promontory had never been rounded, although Catalan ships had certainly passed it less than a century before. Imagination pictured great dangers lying beyond Bojador, and it was believed that no vessel sailing around it could return. Not until 1434 did Henry succeed in persuading one of his captains to double the much-feared cape, but once past it the mariners found calm weather and a placid sea. Henry, much encouraged, pushed his captains on.

Below Cape Bojador they came to an inlet they named River of Gold (Rio de Ouro) from the half-legendary river reported in earlier times, a river probably to be identified with the Senegal, much farther south. Since Rio de Ouro is not a river and produces no gold, the discoverers soon realized their mistake and continued the southward search. It was slow work, for the ships seldom ventured far from the coast and invariably turned back after exploring a few miles beyond the limits reached by their predecessors.

The greatest advance down the west African coast in Henry's time came in the decade of the 1440's. In those years the prince's ships passed Cape Verde and discovered the mouths of the Senegal and Gambia. For the rest of Henry's days the Portuguese captains never pressed far south of those rivers, although one of them sighted the impressive range of mountains called Sierra Leone. Their immediate and main interest became the exploration of the rivers in quest of Christians and gold. Some gold they found, because the old reports they followed had a grain of truth. Christians were of course out of the question, since Prester John's Abyssinia lay on the other side of the African continent. But rumors of Christians persisted, and the natives cheerfully co-operated by revising what little they knew of the interior to correspond with the kind of information they soon found was wanted.

Meanwhile the Portuguese traded along the coast and up the rivers and eked out their profits with cargoes of fish and sealskins. In a limited way they began the modern African slave trade, carrying back to Portugal a few Negroes originally received as presents from friendly native rulers. The traffic at first amounted to little, since Portugal had small use for slaves in the fifteenth century. Later, following the Spanish discovery of America and the development of the Portuguese Atlantic islands, the human cargoes became large and economically profitable.

The last important discovery made in Prince Henry's lifetime was that of the Cape Verde Islands. Alvise da Cadamosto, a Venetian in the prince's service who was sailing for the Gambia, sighted several of the eastern members of the group in 1457. The Cape Verdes were uninhabited and hence offered the Portuguese a new colonizing opportunity.

Henry died in 1460 at the age of sixty-six. Although the events of his life are fully known, we have next to no information regarding his personality. His official biographer portrayed him as a somber, ascetic man, solely concerned with his great plans of discovery. No doubt this portrait applies better to Henry's later years than to his youth, when he appears to have been a gallant who partook of the pleasures and frivolities of the era. There can be no doubt of the tremendous importance of his work. Though the extent of his plans and aspirations is frequently exaggerated, one may still call him the greatest figure in the history of exploration. Certainly he was the first man who devoted his life to patronizing discovery and to gathering geographical data. Even though he had no grandiose plan for rounding Africa and approaching the East through the Indian Ocean, his work ultimately suggested the idea to others. His very failure to reach Prester John and a supply of gold by the southern water route forced his successors to pursue and modify the plan.

King John II

Over twenty years elapsed between Henry's death and the reign of his grandnephew John II (1481–1495), who was the next royal patron of discovery. Even though the Portuguese government neglected Africa during the intervening years, exploration still went on. Private merchants, foreign as well as Portuguese, sought a share in the trade of Guinea, as the whole west African coast was then coming to be called. From 1469 to 1474 the government gave the trade monopoly there to Fernão Gomes, on condition that he send out exploring as well as trading expeditions.

Gomes faithfully kept his part of the bargain. Besides bringing back cargoes of slaves, ivory, gold dust, and melegueta pepper, he sent his ships eastward along the Gold, Ivory, and Slave Coasts and around the bend at the Cameroons almost to the mouth of the Congo. But for all Gomes' energy, the contract was not renewed, because the vigorous young Prince John decided that the African enterprise should return to royal hands.

The prince was unable to push the exploration effectively until the death of his romantic and ineffectual father, Afonso V, made him king of Portugal in 1481. Then, although harassed by the conspiracies of his great nobles, who were determined to kill him, he found time and resources to outfit an African expedition. This succeeded in establishing a fort and trading post at Mina on the Gold Coast which could serve as a base for further explorations. Like Prince Henry, John had hoped to reach Prester John from some point in West Africa, but already he had greater ideas. India was now what interested him. Though the geographical riddle of the Dark Continent had not been solved, John already guessed the answer and was prepared to gamble that Africa could be rounded.

It did not take him long to act. In 1482 and again in 1484 he sent out Diogo Cão, a brave and experienced commander, to push as far as possible to the south. The timid advances of Prince Henry's day were a thing of the past now, and the Portuguese advanced by giant strides. On his first expedition, Cão discovered the mouth of the Congo River, being guided to it by the mud and vegetation the mighty stream poured into the Atlantic. After exploring far down the coast of Angola, he returned to the Congo, where he picked up several hostages who were subjects of the Mani Congo, an interesting African prince who ruled in pomp and style a few miles up the river. Cão took these Negroes to Portugal, where the king gave them Christian baptism and a thorough briefing not only regarding his plans but their own role therein. The Congolese were particularly urged to be alert for any word of Christians to the east and to pass on such information to the next white men (naturally Portuguese) whom they met.

On his second trip to Africa, Cão restored the Congo natives to their people and then, leaving the river once more, pushed far beyond the limit of his first voyage to Cape Cross in what today is Southwest Africa. Some unexplained circumstance, perhaps the commander's death, caused the Portuguese to halt at the cape and then return. John, however, felt that his next voyager would make a great discovery.

The Route to India

Having by now solved the problem of his rebellious nobles by killing the ringleaders, the king could proceed unhampered to the solution of his other great problem, Africa. The continent, though still important to him, had become largely the means to an end, and the end was India. In order to examine the problem from both sides, John prepared two expeditions for the year 1487. He began by sending two Arabic-speaking Portuguese across the Mediterranean, to go from North Africa to India and Prester John's Abyssinia. One scout soon died, but the other, Pero de Covilhã, managed to visit all lands assigned to both. After reaching India, he returned to Cairo and from there sent back a letter informing King John that the most promising trading port in India was Calicut on the coast of Malabar. Covilhã then entered Abyssinia, where the ruler somehow failed to recognize himself in the role of Prester John, and, taking the Portuguese visitor for a spy, refused to let him leave the country.

King John's other expedition, commanded by Bartolomeu Dias, set out in a small fleet with orders to pass Diogo Cão's farthest point and if possible to turn the tip of Africa. Dias accomplished his mission. After being driven below the southern limit of the continent by storms, the ships touched Africa again east of the cape. The brave commander then persuaded the weary and homesick seamen to continue sailing east until the northward bend of the continent clearly showed that they were entering the Indian Ocean. Not until their homeward voyage did the Portuguese explorers finally see the mighty cape near the southern end of Africa. The name Good Hope was given by the king in recognition of the boundless prospects opened by its discovery.

By the end of 1488 King John had learned the two things he needed most to know. Africa ended about 36° S., and beyond that lay the open route to India. But though the king lived and reigned another seven years, his elaborate preparations for a new voyage were not completed by the time of his death. Dias had reported that the lateen-rigged caravels, in which most of the previous expeditions, including his own, had sailed, were too light, too fragile, and too low in the water to navigate the turbulent waters of the cape and the southern Atlantic. Instead, he recommended *naus*, a heavier rounder type of ship with square rigging and a greater draft. Slower though they were, *naus* would be more seaworthy in those waters and would provide more space for seamen's quarters and provisions. Almost at once, on royal orders, Dias set to work supervising the construction of proper *naus*, the ships that would bear Vasco da Gama to India.

Treaty of Tordesillas

In 1493 Christopher Columbus, returning from the discovery of America, was driven into Lisbon by bad weather. He underwent a thorough questioning from John, and although the Portuguese ruler doubted that Columbus had been to Marco Polo's Cipangu (first identified with Haiti), he did feel that the new explorations in the names of Ferdinand and Isabella represented something dangerous to Portuguese ambitions. John coolly claimed that all the western lands belonged to him; Columbus and his Spanish sovereigns rushed a message to Rome appealing to the pope. Alexander VI was himself a Spaniard and on much better terms with Castile and Aragon than with Portugal. He issued a series of bulls during the year designed to reinforce the claims of the Spanish rulers to any new lands they wanted, east or west. John, paying slight heed to this papal interference, let his Spanish neighbors know that he was prepared to fight unless he got a better settlement. Though reluctant to make concessions, Ferdinand and Isabella finally yielded and in June of 1494 signed the Treaty of Tordesillas with the emissaries of Portugal. This agreement divided the spheres of exploration by an imaginary line drawn from pole to pole through the Atlantic 370 leagues west of the Cape Verde Islands, approximately where the forty-sixth meridian of longitude runs. East of the line Portugal gained full and exclusive rights to discovery and conquest, and Spain (or rather Castile) received the same privileges to the west.

Roughly, King John and his descendants received the Eastern Hemisphere and the Spanish monarchs the Western, except for the shoulder of Brazil that turned out to lie on the Portuguese side, and part of Australia and the east Asian coast, which went to Spain. Neither country proved overly scrupulous in abiding by the agreement, but in general it proved workable for them until the eighteenth century. Since the pope later gave his blessing to the pact, other Catholic countries were obliged to pay some attention to it, although Protestant states felt no such obligation.

Vasco da Gama

King John died late in 1495 without sending an expedition to India, which the treaty awarded to him. His brother-in-law and successor Manuel I (1495–1521), better known as Manuel the Fortunate, lacked John's ability but was energetic and determined to carry out the plan. The new king spent the year 1496 in regulating home affairs, particularly in arranging for the expulsion or forced conversion of the Portuguese Jews, a policy destined to prove damaging to his country later. But by 1497 all was ready for the voyage to India. The new ships built by Dias had been finished and placed under the command of a little-known member of the Portuguese nobility, Vasco da Gama. This Da Gama, whose fortune it was to initiate direct European contact with the East, was a man of iron physique and surly disposition. Unlettered, brutal, and violent, he was nevertheless loyal and fearless. For some assignments he would have been useless, but for this one he was made to order. The work lying ahead could not be accomplished by a gentle leader.

On July 18, 1497, Vasco da Gama took his four ships across the bar of the Tagus and, after dropping down to the long-familiar Cape Verde Islands, made a daring innovation. His predecessors—Cão, Dias, and the rest—had merely coasted Africa, seldom venturing far from shore, but Da Gama, after leaving the Cape Verdes, described a huge semi-circle in the South Atlantic and swung over almost to the Brazilian coast. On reaching the higher southern latitudes he encountered the west winds that blew him eastward until he sighted land at St. Helena Bay, a few miles north of the Cape of Good Hope. Rounding the cape, he sailed into the Indian Ocean and up the east coast of Africa, through waters never before cut by a European keel.

The first Arabs they met cordially received the Portuguese strangers; but on learning that they were Christians, the Moslems quickly guessed that their guests would prove dangerous, and friendship chilled to open hostility. The Portuguese luckily avoided several traps laid for them and continued their northward cruise. Not until reaching Malindi, a city in the modern Kenya territory, did they find a warmer welcome. There a sultan, who for local political reasons decided to befriend the strangers, even provided Da Gama with a pilot to guide him to Calicut, the goal of the Portuguese ever since Pero de Covilhã's letter to John II.

Reaching Calicut in 1498, Vasco da Gama found a Hindu ruler who seemed utterly unimpressed with him and his bedraggled expedition. The Portuguese bargained for spices, although they had little to offer in trade, since the Indians turned up their noses at the few European goods they had brought. Da Gama, after displaying what for him was unusual patience, managed finally to stock his holds with a slim cargo of spices and other oriental luxuries. Then, avoiding an armed clash with Arab traders, who scented the danger his pioneering expedition offered and wished to destroy it, he sailed for home. One of his four ships had been broken up during the outward voyage; another had to be abandoned and burned on the way back, as sickness took a steady toll of the dwindling crews. The remaining two vessels finally reached Lisbon in the summer of 1499.

Aftermath of the Voyage

This voyage is one of the landmarks of world history. It established, for the first time, direct sea communication between the Occident and the Orient, thereby opening the fabled East and its treasures to the cupidity and daring of the West. Portugal could anticipate immediate wealth, and King Manuel loudly trumpeted his joy, but in the long run all Europe stood to profit from this epoch-making feat.

As an achievement of exploration, however, the voyage had definite limitations. Dias had already proved that Africa could be rounded; the Indian Ocean had been sailed by civilized Asiatics for centuries; and the great voyage failed, for the moment at least, to change Europe's concept of the eastern ocean and of Hindustan. Ptolemy still held sway there for several years, and his erroneous map was copied by some European cartographers long after the Portuguese had revealed its obsolescence. But these mossbacks gradually abandoned the field, for science now was truly on the march.

CHAPTER IV

Portugal Rules the East

THE extent of Portugal's diplomatic victory at Tordesillas could now be seen by all. When Vasco da Gama returned from Calicut, Spain's admiral, Columbus, had for several years been fumbling among the West Indian Islands, under the fond impression that he was in the Far East. Already Spaniards had lost their first enthusiasm for these places, which had seemed to promise so much and had actually yielded so little. Now King Manuel's voyager had been to lands that everyone knew were the real East. And the beauty of it was that Portugal by the treaty had forever shut her rival out of this long-coveted oriental sphere.

Discovery of Brazil

Eagerly preparations were made in Lisbon to exploit the contact gained with India. In 1500 Pedro Álvares Cabral sailed with a fleet of thirteen ships. Partly following Da Gama's course in the South Atlantic, but swinging farther west, Cabral struck the Brazilian coast in the region of Porto Seguro. Swarms of naked savages came to greet the Europeans, to look on in wonder as the expedition's chaplains celebrated the first Catholic mass on Brazilian soil. It was instantly realized that this land lay east of the Tordesillas line and so belonged to Portugal. Cabral sent one ship back to Lisbon to report the new discovery and with the rest of the fleet proceeded according to orders to India. After losing several ships in a storm, he finally rounded the Cape of Good Hope and, while proceeding up the eastern side of Africa, discovered the important island of Madagascar. Cabral then cruised along the western coast of India, alternately trading with the Indians and fighting with the Arab shippers, who would not tamely surrender to Europeans their monopoly of Indian Ocean trade. He returned to Portugal with a spice cargo but minus so many ships that the whole voyage showed a loss.

For a moment Portugal seemed to hesitate. There were even persons who urged King Manuel to abandon the India adventure, which seemed beyond the power and resources of Portugal. But any hesitation was brief; the king's decision was to see the matter through.

Founding the Empire

During the next few years, the Portuguese made annual expeditions to India. At first they went only for trade, but in 1505 they began a policy of building fortifications and dominating the local princes. Because India was then divided and without great military states, the handful of European invaders were able to establish themselves firmly on the shores of the Indian Ocean before a wave of Turkish conquerors came from beyond the Khyber Pass to build the powerful Mogul Empire that ultimately included most of Hindustan.

Meanwhile, the Portuguese learned eastern geography and the timing of the monsoons that would blow them from East Africa to India. They also learned the routes and centers of trade—that the city of Malacca was the great spice market at the eastern end of the Indian Ocean and that Ormuz and Aden commanded the entrances to the Persian Gulf and the Red Sea. They came to know the true shape of Hindustan and something of the Malay Peninsula beyond. East Africa was strategically important to them, and they soon mapped the entire coast from the cape to the Red Sea.

Under Afonso de Albuquerque, King Manuel's greatest commander and governor in the East, the Portuguese definitely advanced from trade to empire building. This grizzled veteran, with a long career as a European soldier behind him, was aged almost sixty when sent out by his sovereign to manage Portuguese oriental affairs in 1509. It was Albuquerque who most truly appreciated the fact that Portugal could accomplish nothing without solid bases on land. During the six years (1509–1515) that he governed for his king, he strove to conquer the key points of the Indian Ocean, in order to squeeze out competition and render Portugal's hold invulnerable. Quick in action and ruthless in punishment, he spared neither refractory natives nor rebellious Portuguese. Frequently suffering from illness and the infirmities of age, he dominated the ocean by his iron will and left a reputation that four and a half centuries have scarcely effaced.

On the west coast of Hindustan, he took Goa to serve as the center of Portuguese power. To the east he seized Malacca, which controlled the entry of East Indian spices and other goods to the Indian Ocean. Farther west he captured Muscat and Ormuz, which dominated the Persian Gulf, and made it possible to close that important route to Europe. It was only in his attempt to capture Aden that he failed; here he was beaten off and in consequence could not bar the entrance to the Red Sea, which carried the greatest spice supply of all. If Aden had fallen, Portugal might have diverted the whole trade around the Cape of Good Hope and gained a total monopoly. As it was, the ancient republic of Venice, aroused to the situation, made every effort to keep the Red Sea open and the old spice trade alive. Then in 1517 the Ottoman Turks conquered Egypt and acquired not only the old route but the Egyptian interest in the revenue from this trade. With Venetian encouragement the Turks kept some eastern commerce flowing through the Red Sea and along the various overland routes as in the years before the Portuguese rounded Africa.

Portugal in the Far East

Albuquerque was responsible for his nation's first push into the East Indian Archipelago, the Pacific, and the Far East. After his conquest of Malacca in 1511, he sent a fleet beyond the Malaccan Strait to the Banda and Molucca Islands in quest of the nutmeg and clove which came from these distant places. The commander of this expedition, Antonio de Abreu, can truly be called the discoverer of the Pacific, since he entered the mighty ocean in 1512, months before Balboa sighted it from the peak in Darien. Abreu himself turned back at the Bandas, but one of his officers, Francisco Serrão, reached Ternate in the Moluccas, where he spent the rest of his life. It was he who, in a letter, put into the head of his friend, Ferdinand Magellan, the idea that the Moluccas, richest of all the spice islands, lay over 180° east of the Tordesillas line and so belonged to Castile instead of Portugal. Serrão proved to be mistaken, but his error had a substantial impact on the course of future discovery.

Albuquerque established contact with Siam and Java; the Portuguese soon coasted Formosa and in 1514 succeeded in getting an agent to Canton. By 1542 a group of them had made a visit to Japan, and in 1557 their country acquired the lease of Macau, the oldest European possession in China.

Prester John Again

The search for Prester John had by now slipped a little into the background, but Portugal did not entirely forget the earliest objective of her explorations. A Portuguese mission visited Abyssinia in 1520 and brought back a description that reduced the Prester's celebrated empire to the status of another backward African kingdom. It was Christian, however—the old report had contained that much truth. Pero de Covilhã, King John's former emissary, who had been marooned in Abyssinia for thirty years, was still alive and glad to see his countrymen, even though he refused their invitation to accompany them home. He decided that he would now be an utter stranger in Portugal and foresaw complications as the result of having left one wife and family there and of having since acquired another in Abyssinia. The curtain now fell forever on this stalwart pioneer, as the Portuguese left the patriarch amid the rugged African mountains to be buried at some future date with different Christian rites from those of Catholic Portugal.

The Profits Fade Away

For all her effort, Portugal never gained effective mastery of the Indian Ocean. Her navy and merchant marine, though large by the standards of the sixteenth century, were small in relation to the enormous water area and its almost endless coasts. Some dozen ships a year ordinarily rounded the cape from Portugal, and many of these straightway returned with cargoes, leaving a small resident force to contend with the ever-present enemies in the East. Though repeatedly defeated by the Portuguese, these enemies always rose again to baffle the lesser men who succeeded the great Albuquerque after his death in 1515.

For the first few years the Portuguese seemed to be making enormous profits from their eastern trade. Private fortunes did mushroom, the king's chests did swell, and Lisbon took on an air of luxury and ostentation. But as Portugal expanded in the East, expenses tended to outrun the revenue, and soon most of the profit faded away. Many costly ships were lost; forts and trading posts required large investments; governors had to be well paid, and many—with their subordinates—found grafting so easy that the royal treasury suffered.

The Portuguese, though unrivaled as explorers and pioneers, never became able merchants. Their small, poor country had previously been mainly agricultural and had never produced a substantial middle class. The persecution of the Jews on the eve of Da Gama's voyage crippled the one group that might have risen economically to the new occasion. To replace them, the bankers of Italy, Belgium, and Germany seized the opportunity for investment and drew most of the profits from the eastern trade.

It also turned out that Lisbon, though excellent as a point of departure for the distant voyages, was neither a good center of distribution nor an adequate market. It lay too far from the main trading centers of the continent, too far from the well-to-do Europeans who could buy the luxury products Portugal now had to offer. Antwerp served the purpose much better, and within a few years this city on the Scheldt had nearly supplanted the city by the Tagus. The Portuguese brought their spices from the East to Lisbon, only to have most of the cargoes sent on to Antwerp at once. Later, with the rise of the Dutch Republic, Amsterdam superseded Antwerp as the focus of European eastern trade.

Portugal held grimly to her oriental empire through the sixteenth century and on into the seventeenth, but in the long run held a losing hand. Albuquerque had been right in deciding that the Portuguese could dominate the trade only by building a land base, but he did not foresee that an eastern empire would become a dead weight on his tiny nation. Gallant the Portuguese had indeed been in blazing the trail into the unknown, and as Camões, their poet, says, "if there had been more world they would have found it." But when commercial skills and energies were called for, Portugal began, slowly but inevitably, to revert to the humble position dictated by geography, poverty, and lack of manpower.

For a brief historical moment the Portuguese had astonished the world, and the importance of their work has never been clearer than it is today.

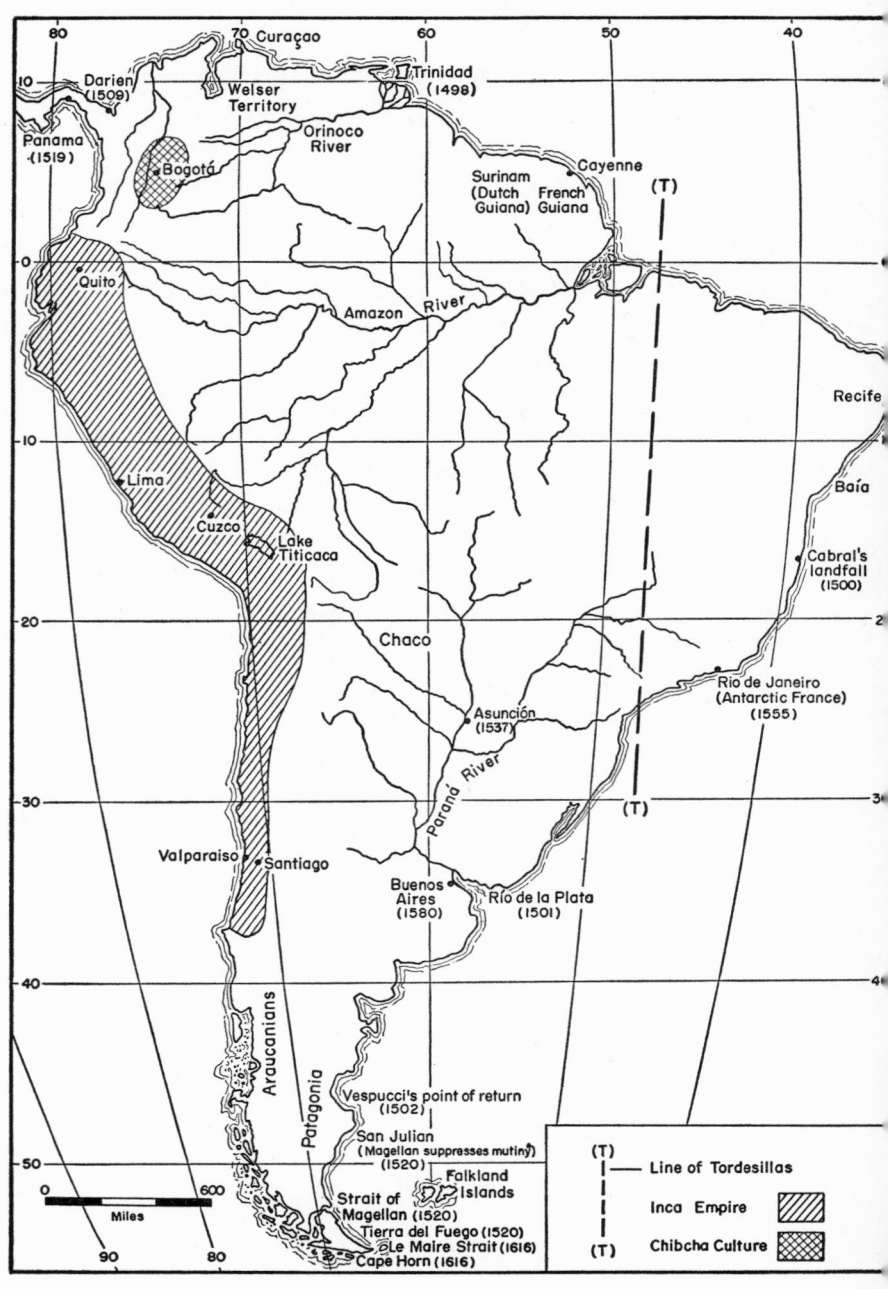

European explorations and settlements in South America.

CHAPTER V

Spain and the West~~~~~~

SPAIN started overseas discovery later than Portugal. Not until the marriage of Ferdinand and Isabella in 1469 were the two main Spanish kingdoms of Aragon and Castile finally united, and not until the capture of Granada in 1492 was the last Moslem stronghold in the peninsula destroyed. But long before the Spaniards could turn their attention to distant adventure, they were developing qualifications for their future work as empire builders. The seaports of Biscay, Galicia, and Andalusia produced good seamen. Centuries of fighting with the Moors and with one another had endowed the Spaniards with a proud bravery and a religious fanaticism which were to serve them well when they bore the cross against the new unbelievers overseas. While recovering their peninsula and the Balearic Islands from the Moors, the Spaniards had gained some experience in dealing with subject peoples. Since 1402, when the Castilians had begun the conquest of the Canary Islands, they had faced, on a miniature scale, many of the problems they were to encounter in the New World. Even so, until Columbus appeared at the Spanish court, there was small reason to think that Spain was about to carve out a vast empire in unknown lands.

Christopher Columbus

There is no point in adding here to the debates regarding the origin and birthplace of Christopher Columbus. He was born, it would appear, in 1451. He called himself a Genoese Italian, and in his lifetime no one seems to have doubted his word, though in recent years many nations have claimed him as their own. Early in life he left Genoa and sailed on ships in both the Mediterranean and the Atlantic, visiting England certainly and perhaps reaching the latitude of Iceland. He married the daughter of the wealthy Portuguese donatary of Porto Santo, an island in the Madeira group, and after her death moved to Lisbon to make plans for a westward voyage of discovery in the Atlantic. He collected stories of lands to the west, including the curious legend of Antilia, which was supposed to be a rich and luxurious island populated by Christians who had once migrated there from Europe. Confused reports of the Norse Greenland colony may have provided the basis of the Antilia myth and in this way have furnished indirectly the only influence the Scandinavian voyages could have had on the discovery of America. Columbus already knew about Marco Polo's book by hearsay, even though he did not read it until later. What interested him most was the account of Cipangu (Japan), which Polo had never visited but described as very rich, and of Cathay, the home of the Great Khan.

Columbus believed the earth to be a sphere, though that made no significant contribution to his plans, since everybody of any learning believed the same. More important are the facts that he underestimated the circumference of the globe and simultaneously exaggerated the size and eastward extension of Asia. These miscalculations combined to place the east coast of Asia much nearer the west coast of Europe than it actually is. Columbus' errors, plus Marco Polo's mistake in locating Japan too far east of China, promised a relatively short voyage to golden Cipangu. Along the way, moreover, the pleasant island of Antilia could be expected to break the journey.

These misconceptions were further reinforced by a letter which the Florentine scientist Paolo dal Pozzo Toscanelli had a little earlier written to a Lisbon priest and which somehow fell into Columbus' hands. The scientist not only rehashed familiar stories and legends and reached the convenient conclusion that a voyage from Europe to Cipangu and Cathay would prove easy; he also recalled that Kublai Khan had once expressed an interest in Christianity and had asked the elder Polos to bring missionaries back to China. All in all the document represented more wishful thinking than Florentine science, but it seems to have helped Columbus somewhat in clarifying his ideas.

About 1484 Columbus asked John II of Portugal to send him on a voyage of discovery to the west. After some consideration, the king turned the proposal down. Columbus, though an impressive-looking man who talked well, came of a poor family and had little formal education. These facts were perhaps apparent to the king and to the Portuguese scientists who discussed the plan with him. The price Columbus demanded for his services was high, and King John was just then awaiting the return of Diogo Cão from the Congo and had a heavy commitment to reach India by rounding Africa. The vulgar and ridiculous opinion has persisted, however, that John was dissuaded by the fear that his ships might fall off the edge of a flat earth.

Columbus next carried his proposal to the court of Spain.

Everyone knows he had to wait nearly seven years; not everyone knows that from the start he had powerful friends to urge his cause. The ingratitude of Spain toward Columbus, which is a part of our modern tradition, is an idea originally implanted by the discoverer himself. He had a persecution complex, and his last complaining letters, written near his death when he was discouraged and sick, show far greater remembrance of his detractors than of his many loyal friends and supporters.

When Moorish Granada fell in January 1492, the tide of royal favor turned quickly in his direction; the money was somehow raised, although the story that Queen Isabella pawned her jewels to help Columbus is untrue; they had already been pawned for another purpose. Even Columbus' extreme demands for rewards and titles were accepted. At the little port of Palos the famous *Santa Maria*, *Pinta*, and *Niña* were fitted out and manned with crews numbering about 120 all told. Less certainty exists about the architecture and equipage of this fleet than is sometimes loosely supposed. The *Niña* was certainly the smallest, the *Pinta* the fastest, and the *Santa Maria* the heaviest and slowest. All three vessels were caravels, though varying somewhat as to rigging; the *Niña* had lateen (triangular) sails, while the *Santa Maria* and *Pinta* bore square ones except for their mizzen masts, which were lateen rigged.

The Discovery of America

Leaving Palos in August 1492, Columbus touched at the Canaries long enough to repair slight damages to the *Pinta* and then sailed westward into the Atlantic. Although there was grumbling aboard the *Santa Maria*, no serious case of mutiny occurred, and the voyagers enjoyed the finest weather. The historic landfall at Guanahani (San Salvador) took place on October 12, according to the log of the expedition which says:

> Soon they saw naked people, and the Admiral [Columbus] went ashore in the armed ship's boat, with Martín Alonso Pinzón and his brother Vicente Yáñez. . . . Stepping ashore they saw very green trees and many streams, as well as fruits of different varieties. . . . They took possession for the King and Queen their Lords, with all the customary formalities.

Since Columbus calculated he had already passed Antilia, he cruised southward through the Bahamas to Cuba, which he took to be a part of Cathay, the home of the Great Khan. No Khan was forthcoming to be sure, but the discoverer consoled himself with the thought that this powerful ruler would soon be found. Next the expedition turned eastward and explored the northern coast of Haiti. (The name Haiti will be used here for the entire island, which includes the modern Haitian and Dominican Republics. Haiti is the original Indian name, and although Hispaniola is technically correct, it is somewhat archaic today.) The assumption that Haiti must be Cipangu was strengthened in Columbus' mind by the gold trinkets the Indians wore.

Clumsy work by the pilots wrecked the flagship *Santa Maria* on the Haitian coast. Since no lives were lost, the admiral, for Columbus now bore this title, founded a small colony called Navidad with the surplus men, and then returned to Europe with his remaining ships. Columbus, in the *Niña*, made a brief stop at the Azores and next was compelled by heavy weather to sail into the Tagus and anchor near Lisbon. He could evidently not resist the temptation to strut a little in the presence of King John. The Portuguese monarch listened to the story of the man he had rebuffed less than a decade before, asked many questions, and then made his astonishing claim to ownership of all the new lands. Columbus, taking alarm, rushed an overland messenger to warn Ferdinand and Isabella. The Spanish rulers, as already mentioned, in their turn, rushed an appeal to Pope Alexander to support their claims. Thus began the diplomatic maneuverings that ended in the Treaty of Tordesillas and its line of demarcation.

Columbus had a brief spell of glory on his return to Spain; his royal patrons accepted all his theories about the discovery of Cipangu and Cathay and overlooked the fact that beyond a few trinkets and gewgaws he had no wealth to show. A few American Indians, brought as exhibits, aroused great interest. Being obviously human and yet unlike any men Europeans had seen before, these strange creatures were easily accepted as having come from the Orient.

Later Voyages of Columbus

In September 1493 the admiral, at the head of a large, well-manned expedition, sailed west again, this time by a more southerly route which took him through the Lesser Antilles, a name derived from that of the old legendary Antilia. Discovering Puerto Rico, he made his way to Haiti, only to find that his colonists at Navidad had disappeared—killed, as he later learned, by the normally peaceful natives, who had been goaded to this violence by Spanish cruelty.

After founding a new colony farther east along the coast, Columbus quickly put to sea again, determined to prove that Cuba was part of mainland Asia and the empire of the Great Khan. Coasting the southern shore, with a side expedition to Jamaica, he followed the Cuban coast almost to its western limit. Having stopped just short of proving it an island, he made his officers and crews take a solemn oath that they believed they were following the Asiatic mainland. With his own confidence thus buttressed, he returned to Haiti to explore the interior for gold and slaves. He found no gold worth mentioning but did ship a few cargoes of natives to Spain, where they proved utterly unsatisfactory as laborers. Feeling his influence with the Spanish rulers to be ebbing, Columbus returned in 1496 to try to win their confidence again.

Since this is not a biography of the admiral, it only remains to summarize his two last voyages. Ferdinand and Isabella still had faith or hope enough to send him out in 1498 with a fair-sized expedition. He approached America on this third occasion from the Cape Verde Islands, and discovered Trinidad and the adjacent Venezuelan coast. Venezuela had pearl fisheries, the best source of ready wealth the Spaniards had thus far found. Though Columbus scarcely knew what to make of the mainland, he recognized its continental character. Somewhere to the west, he reasoned, there must be a strait between this great land and the Malay Peninsula he had seen on the maps modeled after Ptolemy. Ptolemy's original map did not show a strait, for on it the Indian Ocean was a landlocked sea. But this idea had been corrected by Marco Polo and others who had gone by water around Malaya from China to India. This strait, Columbus thought, would lead into the Indian Ocean. But he could not seek the strait just then and had to postpone the search until his fourth voyage, which began in 1502. On this last expedition, he sailed from Spain to find the strait and by means of it the route to southern Asia. With this end in view he explored the coasts of Central America and the Isthmus of Panama, thinking that he was following Ptolemy's Malay Peninsula. From the Indians he learned of the Pacific, not far away, and judged it to be the eastern Indian Ocean, which Ptolemy called the *Sinus Magnus*. Finally, however, he reached and passed the point where the isthmus joins South America. No strait had appeared, so something was obviously wrong with the theory. Columbus now revised his calculations to fit the newest facts. His last opinion was that the Malay Peninsula extended farther south than he had first supposed and that South America was part of it. This meant that the passage into the Indian Ocean must be sought far to the south, because by now other voyagers had traced the continent well into the Southern Hemisphere.

The admiral, whose health had failed, could make no more voyages and was almost forgotten until his death in 1506. Queen Isabella had died in 1504, and Ferdinand, who survived her, had lost interest in discovery, but the story that Columbus died in poverty is a legend. His final will and testament shows that he divided a substantial amount of property among his heirs.

Amerigo Vespucci

Other explorers had taken up the work of Columbus and, even before his death, had made substantial progress. By a series of coasting voyages, the Spaniards closed up the huge gap between the part of Brazil discovered by Cabral for Portugal in 1500 and the last points reached by Columbus along the Isthmus. They found many breaks and indentations in the mainland, but nothing that on investigation proved to be a strait. Then came the Florentine Amerigo Vespucci (1454–1512) to give new shape and meaning to these ill-digested findings.

Vespucci, trained from his youth in the Medici Bank of Florence, was directing his firm's office in Seville when the Spanish explorations first began. Moved by the great discoveries across the ocean, he left loans and discounts for navigation, and with his high intelligence and sound mathematical training became the best geographer and cosmographer of his time. Sailing in the service of both Spain and Portugal, he took part in a number of voyages, the most important being with the Portuguese expedition of 1501–1502, which King Manuel sent to follow up Cabral's discovery of Brazil. Vespucci sailed past the present limit of Brazil, discovered the Río de la Plata, and turned back at some point on the Patagonian coast. Though the voyagers did not quite reach the end of South America, Vespucci felt sure that a little farther on a strait would be found leading through the continent.

Amerigo described the new lands he had seen in letters to friends which became famous throughout Europe. Versions in several languages had been printed before his death, and from what we can learn, the public bought each edition as fast as it left the press. In one of these letters he called the South American land mass *Mundus Novus* (New World) thereby registering his conviction that it bore no resemblance to any region described by ancient writers. In 1507 a mediocre German geographer, Martin Waldseemüller, in a rather amateurish scientific treatise proposed that this new world be named after Amerigo, whom he supposed to be its discoverer. Waldseemüller even prepared a map in which the area of Brazil was labeled America. His effort to name the western continent failed to attract much immediate attention; gradually, however, the word America came to be used more often, possibly because it had a pleasant sound. In 1541 the famous geographer Gerardus Mercator made a map of the New World on which he spelled AME across the northern continent and placed RICA across the southern. That as good as settled the issue, though the Iberian countries, where the facts of the discovery were better known, continued to call the New World the "Indies" until the eighteenth century.

Vespucci, after he retired from active voyaging, became pilot major of Spain and in that capacity trained navigators, directed exploration, and fitted the new discoveries into a great official map that was prepared in his office at Seville. Without a doubt it was he who made the discovery of a southern strait the major purpose of later Spanish exploration. Men could see by now that South America hung as an appendage to something, presumably to the continent of Asia, although the little they knew of North America did seem strangely uninviting by contrast with what Marco Polo had led them to expect. The two Cabots had explored the northern coasts for England and had found nothing profitable or promising. Clearly the Spice Islands and the rich Indian Ocean regions lay beyond the enormous land bulk that blocked the Spaniards in every latitude. To reach the Indian Ocean a way through the barrier was needed, so Vespucci's theory of a southern strait was taken up and tested by Juan Díaz de Solís and Ferdinand Magellan.

Solís and Magellan

On Amerigo's death Solís succeeded him as pilot major and in 1515 set out in command of an expedition to find this southern strait and a western route to the islands that Portugal was now exploiting in the East. Solís coasted southward along Brazil, passed the Tordesillas demarcation line, and proceeded into the Spanish sphere as far as the Río de la Plata. Even though Vespucci had found and explored the great estuary years before, Solís turned in to investigate. Somewhere in the present territory of Uruguay he landed with a small party, only to be slaughtered by the arrows of the inhospitable Charrúa Indians, who according to one version then proceeded to dine off the doughty navigator. His discouraged subordinates at once sailed for home, leaving the real geographical question still unanswered.

The Portuguese Magellan (1480–1521) was the next to take up the search. After serving under Albuquerque and other renowned commanders in the East for several years, he became disgruntled with Portuguese policies and with his own failure to achieve promotion. A letter from his friend Francisco Serrão, then living on Ternate in the Moluccas, convinced him that those valuable spice islands, which Portugal still had not seized, lay in the zone assigned to Castile at Tordesillas and led him to offer his services to Spain. Not only did he have the tempting possession of the Moluccas to offer the Spaniards, but he had what he considered an even greater prize. Portuguese seamen, sailing near the Ryukyu Islands north of Formosa, had brought back exaggerated reports of their riches and civilization. Magellan heard and believed these reports, and somehow identified the Ryukyus with the Old Testament Tarshish and Ophir, from which the ships of Solomon and Hiram of Tyre had brought back their celebrated wealth.

His main problem was to reach these eastern islands by water without crossing the Eastern Hemisphere, which the treaty had assigned to Portugal. He soon adopted the theory of a southern strait, though it is impossible to say how much of the plan he took from Vespucci and Solís and how much he evolved himself. He accepted the now fairly general belief that the Pacific, recently seen from Darien by Balboa, was the eastern arm of the Indian Ocean, since, like others of his time, he did not restrict the Indian Ocean to its actual limits but thought of it as extending eastward past the Moluccas. He believed that the Moluccas lay not far west of the Spanish colonies on the isthmus. Magellan thus failed to take account of the width of the still unexplored Pacific.

In 1517 he arrived in Spain to try his fortunes there. His past career and personal appearance might well have argued against him. There were several flaws in his Portuguese service record; Albuquerque had written a bad report concerning him, and King Manuel considered him a questionable character unworthy of further employment. He looked unprepossessing, being short, squat, and rather ugly; he limped from an old leg wound and had scarcely a coin in his pockets. Despite all handicaps, he was soon to eclipse the fame of Albuquerque and to cost his erstwhile sovereign many sleepless nights.

Magellan first explained his plan to responsible Spanish officials, who hesitated. But the young ruler Charles V, grandson of Ferdinand and Isabella, was attracted by the ambitious idea. He gave an affirmative order and wheels were set in motion to prepare the expedition. Magellan received five ships with suitable equipment and crews. He considered Portuguese seamen generally superior to Spanish, and although there existed some basis for his belief, he enlisted so many that the authorities were obliged to call a halt. With a company finally consisting mostly of Spaniards, he left the port of Sanlúcar in 1519 and headed for South America.

Magellan coasted Brazil, explored the Río de la Plata less fatefully and no more successfully than Solís and passed the first winter in a Patagonian roadstead. Here mutiny flared, not from the sailors but from Spanish officers whose loyalty had been tampered with by certain opponents of Magellan's plan in Spain. The commander, taken by surprise at first, quickly learned which men he could rely on and skillfully used them to regain the upper hand and to restore discipline. He dealt punishment to the ringleaders but pardoned their followers and won most of them over. When the weather turned warmer, he resumed the voyage and soon reached the waterway ever since known as the Strait of Magellan. After a brief hesitation, the voyagers entered the strait and explored its many branches. The southern shore they named Tierra del Fuego, for the many fires seen in the distance by night. These were the campfires of the Fuegan Indians, whom the explorers never saw; they kept out of sight in the daytime.

On emerging into the Pacific, which he named because of its apparent serenity, Magellan had three ships left. One had been wrecked off Patagonia; another, in the hands of still recalcitrant mutineers, had deserted in the strait and returned to Spain. The remaining vessels being in fairly good condition, Magellan was free to seek the Moluccas as well as Tarshish and Ophir. He sailed northward for an unknown distance, probably past the equator, before turning west. An Italian passenger, who kept a journal of the expedition, says the voyagers sighted only two tiny islands in the Pacific before reaching the Marianas. Both proved to be uninhabited and totally barren. The real hardships of the voyage now began. Food ran low, drinking water spoiled, and scurvy prostrated most of the men, there being scarcely enough well hands to work the ships. The death rate was appalling; day after day corpses were committed to the Pacific with whatever slight ceremony the tottering survivors could manage. Rat meat became a luxury and the very maggots that spoiled the dwindling sea biscuit were an article of diet. Brackish and evil-smelling drinking water was avidly consumed, the wine supply having long been exhausted. As month followed month, all thought of mutiny was forgotten; no one had the strength or spirit for it, and the most ignorant sailor could understand that to turn back was hopeless; the only hope of salvation lay in pressing on. The slightest touch of bad weather would have destroyed the fleet during those bitter months, but on that first occasion the Pacific Ocean lived up to its name and remained calm.

Even so, Magellan's expedition was near its last gasp when the inhabited Mariana Islands were sighted. Dark-skinned Micronesian natives darted from shore in their canoes and swarmed aboard the ships, stealing everything they could lay hands on. These light-fingered propensities caused Magellan to name their islands the Ladrones (Thieves). A clash could not be avoided, and the enfeebled Spaniards mustered strength enough to push the islanders off the ships and to follow them ashore and plunder everything edible from a native village. Then, having taught the savages that two could play at the game of thievery, Magellan continued his westward voyage, leaving the Marianas to enjoy for a while longer the isolation that had lasted since the beginning of their inhabitation.

Strengthened by the island food, the Spaniards were able in a few weeks to reach the Philippines. Magellan had a Malayan interpreter aboard, and as he addressed the Filipinos, it could be perceived that some of them understood his words. This meant that the fleet had entered the region generally familiar to the Portuguese; in short, contact had been made with the eastern rim of civilization.

Magellan, hitherto distinguished for his excellent judgment, now committed an act of rashness that cost him his life. After converting a Filipino chieftain to Christianity, he with a few of the Spaniards joined this ally in a war against a neighboring chief. Magellan perished in the combat, and his convert quickly apostatized, killing as many of his new white acquaintances as possible and compelling the rest to depart hastily in the ships.

Electing new leaders, the seamen now went on a rather aimless odyssey about the East Indies, until they finally dropped down to the Moluccas. Since the Portuguese had not yet occupied these islands, the Spaniards could fill their holds with a cargo of spice, even though Magellan's old friend Serrão, their expected intermediary, had recently died. Of the three remaining ships, one was now unseaworthy and had to be burned. Another leaked so badly that it was patched up and sent eastward to try the run across the Pacific to the Spanish isthmus of Darien. The third, the *Victoria*, now commanded by the Biscayan Sebastián de El Cano, was assigned the task of eluding the Portuguese and returning to Spain via the Cape of Good Hope.

The ship bound for Darien, baffled by weather, failed to reach the American coast and turned back to the East Indies, to be captured there by the Portuguese. But El Cano's *Victoria*, in spite of more starvation experiences, completed the circumnavigation of the globe and returned to Sanlúcar in 1522. The eighteen survivors aboard, who included the Italian chronicler, were at first surprised to learn that they had apparently lost a day in their time reckoning. The dis-

crepancy was explained, however, when "a certayne excel-
lente man . . . who was also a greate Philosopher and
Astronomer, answered that it could not otherwyse chaunce
unto them, hauynge sayled three years continually, ever
folowynge the soone towarde the West."

Importance of Magellan's Voyage

The earth had been circled and the width of the Pacific
revealed, even though circumnavigation had not been a part
of Magellan's original plan. Since Pythagoras, men had
known the earth to be round; now the *Victoria*, a smaller
ship than any in Columbus' squadron, had provided a con-
crete demonstration. Men could now have some notion,
however dim, of the true ratio of land to water on the face
of the globe.

The great voyage did not solve all problems or altogether
obliterate traces of past erroneous thinking. Scholars would
not entirely abandon Ptolemy and continued for years to
think of the Pacific as an eastern extension of the Indian
Ocean. Their maps showed Asia bending northeastward
from Malaya and joining America not far north of where
Magellan had crossed the Pacific. In this notion, of course,
there was a crude approximation to the truth, and the voyages of Vitus Bering in the eighteenth century showed that
Asia and North America did in fact miss connection by only
a few miles.

CHAPTER VI

Conquistadors in America

SPANISH explorers and conquistadors were by now beginning to penetrate the New World. By Magellan's time a series of sea expeditions had traced the Gulf of Mexico from Yucatan to Florida and proved that Cuba was an island. Besides the original colony on Haiti, the large Caribbean islands of Puerto Rico, Cuba, and Jamaica were occupied and to some extent settled. Meanwhile, in 1509, a Spanish outpost had been established on the Caribbean side of the Isthmus of Darien. Here the conquistadors had their first sustained contact with mainland Indians and found them somewhat different from the weak and docile inhabitants of the Greater Antilles. They not only resisted conquest more fiercely but revealed much greater powers of survival. In the civilized areas—Mexico, Yucatan, Guatemala, Colombia, Ecuador, and Peru—which the Spaniards were soon to encounter, the conquerors cut huge gaps in the population by the ruthless, destructive invasion. But the Indians, with their high birth rate, filled the gaps and, even though conquered, continued to outnumber their masters and to remain the principal racial element.

Discoveries in North America.

The Isthmus and Central America

Vasco Núñez de Balboa, a cunning young Spaniard with a gentleman's background and some veneer of culture, became the first of the great mainland conquistadors. He began with a shrewd political maneuver in Darien, where he managed to depose the incompetent leaders of the colony and to intrigue his own way to power. Then, knowing that in the eyes of the Spanish government his legal position was shaky, he tried to hold power by finding gold and making important discoveries. Balboa knew how to ingratiate himself with the Indians; in fact he went through the form of marriage with the daughter of an important local chieftain. Thereafter he had the advice and assistance of the natives at his disposal. His desire to accomplish something spectacular caused him in 1513 to undertake the historic march across the isthmus to the Pacific. At that time, before Magellan's voyage had revealed the thousands of miles between Darien and the Spice Islands, or Moluccas, Balboa believed he was close enough to the Portuguese sphere of operations to be racing Afonso de Albuquerque to these and other rich places east of Malacca. But his attention was now deflected southward by the Pacific and by rumors of a great empire to the south "with more gold than there was iron in Biscay." This, of course, was the realm of the Incas, and the probability is that Balboa would have been the conqueror of Peru had he not been judicially murdered in 1519 by the aged and jealous Pedrarias, whom King Ferdinand sent out to replace him.

Pedrarias, though ancient, was by no means decrepit. As greedy as Balboa for fame and riches, this cruel old man left a deep impression on the isthmus and Central America. He moved his headquarters to the Pacific side, where he founded

Panama City and launched expeditions in both directions along the coast. Pedrarias gave his personal attention to the north, and sent exploring parties to Costa Rica and Nicaragua. He can in fact be called the founder of Nicaragua, for he followed his agents northward to build cities and govern the country until his death at the age of more than ninety. Pitiless in his Indian dealings, he was equally without mercy for any Spaniard who became his competitor; Balboa's was not the only Castilian head to fall at his relentless orders.

Mexico

To the north, on the plateau of Mexico, lay the great Indian cities then dominated and partly ruled by the conquering Aztecs. This area had a cultural history extending back at least to the beginning of the Christian era. Its complex and stratified society was based on intelligent and productive agriculture and fostered many useful arts and crafts. Though lacking large domesticated animals, which were everywhere wanting in the New World, and lacking the ability to work iron ore, the Aztecs and their subjects had clearly progressed to an advanced stage of civilization. While hard working, they lived a social life that was generally happy and often carefree, their accurate calendar including many holidays and feast days. Their cities, of stone and adobe, were well built and in cleanliness and sanitation surpassed most European cities of that time. The Aztec capital, the predecessor of Mexico City, was situated on an island surrounded by a lake; causeways and aqueducts from the mainland furnished easy transportation and insured a water supply. Impressive palaces for the nobility and pyramids for religious rites dominated a scene which, for sheer beauty and color, rendered the first Spanish beholders spellbound.

The principal weaknesses of the Aztecs were political and religious. Fanatically brave as warriors, they never devised an adequate system for governing the peoples they conquered. The gloomy and bloodthirsty religion that held them in its grip made their ferocious priests the real rulers of Aztec society. The increasing demands of the cruel gods for human sacrifices caused them to draw an ever-increasing number of victims from their subject peoples. While the method of sacrifice sometimes varied, the usual procedure was to place the naked victim upon an altar at the top of one of the religious pyramids. A priest, using a stone or obsidian knife, slashed open the prisoner's breast and inserted his hand to draw out the bloody and quivering heart. So little time did a sacrifice require that frequently hundreds of these offerings could be made in a day. Aztec theory held it a great honor to be thus offered to a god, yet evidence suggests that most of the prisoners would have dispensed with the honor if possible. Therefore, when the Spaniards arrived in 1519, they found an empire ripe for rebellion against its dominant minority.

Hernando Cortés, landing on the Mexican coast from Cuba with a few hundred Spanish adventurers, soon learned both the strength and weakness of the Aztecs. He played his cards to perfection, making his alliances cleverly and taking advantage of every local superstition and prophecy. He was at first allowed to enter the Aztec capital in peace; there, relying on sheer audacity, he made the Aztec emperor his prisoner. Compelled next by a ferocious uprising to abandon the city, Cortés retreated only as far as the homes of his native allies. From there, after recruiting thousands of Indians and receiving Spanish reinforcements from the West Indies, he returned to Mexico City and laid siege. The Aztecs, rallying around a new emperor, fought with savage fury, but Cortés cut their communications with the mainland and shut off their water supply. Disease and hunger contributed as much as Spanish weapons to the Aztec downfall, and in 1521 Cortés found himself master of the city and in a position to extend Spanish rule over the outlying parts. From Mexico City, now his headquarters and residence, he sent expeditions to the west, south, and north. One invaded Guatemala and subdued its civilized inhabitants, whose culture was only slightly inferior to that of Mexico. Other Spaniards, after years of effort, conquered Yucatan, home of the once-brilliant Maya civilization, which had, however, considerably declined by the time of their arrival.

These Spanish conquests were partly, but only partly, the result of superior weapons. Gunpowder had long been known in Europe, but the conquistadors made only sporadic use of firearms; most of their victories were with cold steel. The horse, an animal never before seen in the New World, gave the Spaniards a far greater psychological advantage than did the few muskets and small cannon they brought. Superior leadership on the white side and lack of unity on the Indian side counted for even more.

The Northern Mirage

For years the mysterious but almost empty lands of the far north dazzled the Spaniards with the promise of riches and marvels. Curious names began to be heard—Amazon Island, the Seven Cities of Cibola, and Golden Quivira—each referring to some imagined wonderland in the unknown north. There was the dream of another Mexico, as rich as the first, or the fountain of youth that the elderly conquistador Juan Ponce de León (John of the Lion's Paunch) sought in Florida in the hope that its magical properties might enable him to repeat the adventures and sins of his early years.

Then, too, there was the hope of a strait, somewhere to the north but more convenient than Magellan's. This hope grew along with the opinion that North America and Asia were separated after all. Asia, the theory now ran, swung far to the east above North America but was divided from it by the Strait of Anian, which offered a passage from the Atlantic to the Pacific. Thus, in an inaccurate way, the existence of Bering Strait was anticipated two centuries before it was discovered.

Most of the early inland explorations of America were treasure hunts or expeditions to find the strait. The northward rush was started by the shipwreck of a party of Spaniards on the Texas coast. Several years later four ragged survivors turned up in Mexico, with tales of hardship at Indian hands and a remarkable account of having walked all the way from Texas. Though they had seen none of the wonders of the north, they had heard stories aplenty and felt sure the fabled riches could be found. They also bore tales of vast herds of wild cattle, which must have been American bison.

Responding to these reports, Hernando de Soto, governor of Cuba, landed on the coast of Florida in 1539 with a splendidly equipped expedition of 600 men and disappeared inland. During the next few years De Soto's party roamed over much of the southeastern United States, finally discovering and crossing the Mississippi River near what is now the northern boundary of the state of Mississippi. A little later the commander died; his followers sank his body in the great river he had discovered and tried to make their way overland to Mexico. Compelled to retreat to the Mississippi, they built crude boats and, still several hundred strong, descended the river and coasted the gulf to a Mexican port.

Other adventurers struck directly north from Mexico. A Franciscan friar returned from a reconnoitering expedition, on which he had been accompanied by a single Moorish slave, and reported having sighted the first of the Seven Cities of Cibola. Always the incorrigible optimist, this friar was prone to make the most of anything he found, but it is likely that he had beheld an Indian town from a distance. The Spanish viceroy who had succeeded Cortés in Mexico took this seriously enough to send out a large expedition under Francisco Vásquez Coronado. At the head of 1,000 Spanish soldiers and Indian auxiliaries, Coronado advanced into Arizona and New Mexico before abandoning hope of finding the Seven Cities. He did reach the place the friar appears to have seen, and found it to be nothing but a dirty Indian village. Meanwhile, a branch of the expedition discovered the Grand Canyon, but the Spaniards had small interest in scenery. Coronado now turned his thoughts toward Golden Quivira and sought it eastward in Texas and then to the northward, finally reaching a wretched Indian village near Wichita, Kansas. Dispirited and suffering from injury, Coronado led his bedraggled forces back to Mexico.

Before his return, however, the viceroy had sent Juan Rodríguez Cabrillo and a small fleet up the Pacific coast with orders to get in touch with the land party if possible and to look for any signs of the Pacific entrance to the great transcontinental strait.

Failing to find either the nonexistent strait or Coronado's

expedition, which was traveling far inland, the seafarers did follow the coast northward to San Diego Bay and then past the forty-second parallel to the Rogue River in Oregon. By the time of their return to Mexico, minus Cabrillo, who died on the voyage, the idea of northern treasure had waned. Many years went by before anyone seriously followed up the claim they had given Spain to California.

South America

In South America, Spanish exploration was both faster and more thorough than in the north. From several directions the continent was pierced by expeditions seeking various goals. But all incentives were reducible to one—the search for wealth. The spell of the legendary and the marvelous worked as well here as in the north; Meta, Omagua, El Dorado, and the City of the Caesars were among the strange names that lured the explorers and conquerors on. Each expedition was an epic in its own right; to do justice to each requires the full narratives of Prescott, Helps, Means, Merriman, and other noted historians who have dealt with these adventures and whose works are available to all.

The Inca Empire

The fame of Peru had reached Balboa on the isthmus, and from the moment its existence became known Peru constituted a major goal for Spanish greed and ambition. The mighty Inca Empire, stretching from southern Colombia to central Chile, represented the culmination of an Andean civilization older than that of western Europe. From their capital, Cuzco, the supreme rulers of the empire governed millions of souls including magnificent builders, skillful craftsmen, and expert farmers. The realm abounded with precious metals, though the Incas had no coinage and valued silver and gold only for their ornamental properties.

The Incas proper were but a conquering minority and their empire had been built with the sword. Most of the inhabitants were subject peoples whose ancestors had achieved advanced civilizations before the days of the empire. This whole Andean culture, being an old one, had perhaps already passed its peak and showed signs of becoming static. It was more sophisticated than the Mexican, and human sacrifice had become almost a thing of the past. A well-organized priesthood directed a religious worship involving many gods, but these dieties were placated by prayers, hymns, and offerings of a harmless nature. Society tended to be socialistic in structure; land ownership rested in the state and every person or family had a well-defined position in the system; a position which was hereditary and could rarely be altered. Inca government was centralized; too centralized for its own good, since the forces of the empire could be paralyzed if the supreme ruler died or became helpless.

Into Peru came a handful of Spaniards in 1532, led by the four Pizarro brothers and dominated by Francisco, the grim and elderly head of the family. Francisco Pizarro had spent years serving under Balboa and Pedrarias on the isthmus, and only now was seizing his chance for fame and fortune. Unlettered and without family background, he quickly showed that native ability could compensate for these deficiencies.

Fortunately for his enterprise, he found the Inca Empire torn by a fratricidal war of succession to the throne. Turning the situation to his own advantage, he posed as arbiter between the two rival brothers. Seizing and holding the successful one, he used this man as a puppet to gain control of the empire for himself and to amass an enormous treasure. Then deeming his victim's usefulness at an end, he invented a flimsy pretext for ordering his execution. The Pizarros had counted their gains too soon, for a dangerous Inca rebellion followed. Hard pressed as they were, the Spaniards held firm; although they were outnumbered a hundred to one their skill as soldiers and their steel proved too much for the badly commanded Inca masses armed only with copper and stone implements. Having restored order, Pizarro could proceed with the work of organizing his conquest, of founding Spanish towns, and of distributing the best Inca lands among his followers.

The conquest of Chile followed as a by-product. Pedro de Valdivia, a subordinate of Pizarro and the ablest professional soldier among the conquistadors, invaded the country and, though finally halted by the fierce Araucanian Indians of the south, had by 1550 made the northern and central districts Spanish territory. Here again the land was parceled among the conquistadors, and as Chile had little gold or silver, the Spaniards exploited local Indian labor and settled to a life of farming. The Araucanians, in their remote southern land, proved an obstacle too great even for conquistadors and held out not merely for generations but for centuries. Possessing no culture worth mentioning, no weapons save the most primitive, and no political organization above the tribal level, they relied for defense upon their fanatical bravery, physical strength, and unbelievable cunning. They surrendered at last to the modernized armies of the Republic of Chile in 1884.

Descent of the Amazon

Other Spanish parties, starting from Peru, took possession of Quito and lesser Indian cities in Ecuador. Gonzalo, the youngest Pizarro brother, crossed the Andes in search of forests where cinnamon was said to grow, but found himself, after months of wandering, on a tributary of the Amazon with a band of starving men. His cousin and chief lieutenant, the opportunistic, one-eyed Francisco de Orellana, was dispatched further downstream by boat to search for food. Whether through premeditated treachery or through inability to reascend the river, Orellana and his fifty followers, after finding some supplies, sailed on down to the mouth of the Amazon and thus became the first white men to cross the South American continent. During the months spent in following the mighty river, the Spaniards encountered many hostile natives, and in one place they found, or thought they had found, warrior women. The region through which they sailed was thus called " Land of the Amazons," and the name Amazon in time was transferred to the river itself. Eventually the wanderers made their way to a Spanish port on the Caribbean, where Orellana sailed for Spain. There he raised an expedition to colonize the shores of the great river; but although he returned, the colony was never founded, and his death caused his survivors to abandon the attempt.

The Chibchas

In the highlands of modern Colombia, around Bogotá, there existed another advanced New World culture, that of the Chibchas. While not as rich as the Aztecs or Incas, the Chibchas were well supplied with jewels and precious metals. One branch of this people, dwelling around Lake Guatabita, had once practiced a religious rite that gave rise to the legend of El Dorado, or Gilded Man. Every year they determined the fitness of their chief for further rule by smearing his naked body with adhesive substance and coating him with gold dust from head to foot. To the accompaniment of chants and prayers by the throngs on shore, priests paddled the chieftain in a raft to the deepest part of the lake and cast him overboard. He had then to rid himself of the gold encumbrance and rise to the surface before drowning, thus winning for another year the right to be the ruler. This custom had been discontinued almost a century earlier, but so deeply had other Indians been impressed that they preserved a garbled report of it until Spanish times. By then El Dorado had come to mean a living man of gold, and it was this rare personage whom the conquistadors sought. What they expected to do with such a curiosity raises speculations better left unuttered.

In 1538 Jiménez de Quesada, a Spanish lawyer turned conquistador, left the Caribbean settlement of Santa Marta to seek supplies for that half-starved colony. Advancing up the Magdalena, continually scourged by sickness and by the attacks of wild animals and hostile Indians, his party finally reached the Chibchas. The reputed courage of this people seemed to evaporate in the presence of the desperate Spaniards, who, though out of gunpowder, rapidly made the conquest with steel alone. Quesada occupied Bogotá, and from the Chibcha cities subsequent Spanish expeditions explored the wild interior of southeastern Colombia.

Venezuela

Columbus, on his third voyage, had discovered the Pearl Coast. Later explorers called the territory Venezuela (Little

Venice) because they found Indian habitations built over water which brought recollections of Italian Venice and its canals. In 1527 the Spanish ruler Charles V leased Venezuela to the German banking house of Welser as security for a debt. For almost twenty years the Welsers had the country to themselves, and the pioneering explorations of the interior were carried on by their employees, who brought such unfamiliar names as Alfinger, Speyer, Von Hutten, and Federmann to the New World. Even against the formidable competition of the Spanish conquistadors, the Welsers won a name for cruelty and ruthless exploitation of the natives. But though they left Venezuela a heap of ruins, they did explore the upper Orinoco hinterland—a region little visited even in recent times—in search of gold and the fabled civilizations of the interior. Finally, to save his property, Charles abrogated the Welser grant, making Venezuela a fairly normal Spanish colony.

The Atlantic Coast

In 1535 the first Spanish settlers of the Río de la Plata founded Buenos Aires, drawn there by false reports of silver. Two years later they built Asunción, up the river in Paraguay, to be nearer the true silver source in Bolivia and Peru. It was from Asunción that the first Spanish expeditions took off across the pampas and the Chaco to learn what lay between the great river and the Andes. Even here the Spaniards sought gold and silver and, finding none, concocted wonder tales for their own stimulation. At least one expedition traversed the pampas in search of the mythical City of the Caesars!

By the Treaty of Tordesillas Portugal had received rights to the Brazilian coast, but during the sixteenth century her people confined their occupation of Brazil to a thin line of settlements located on the various bays and harbors. Portugal had all she could manage in Asia and Africa, hence she did not begin the real exploration of the interior until the seventeenth century.

The Spanish Work in America

The explorers and conquerors sought wealth and marvels, and to them geographical knowledge was distinctly a secondary aim. Yet their greatest significance lies in the amount of New World geography they revealed. Soon after 1550 maps were being drawn that presented not only the recognizable contours of South America but, in spite of many blank spots, the basic features of the interior; the Andes, the Amazon, the Orinoco, the Magdalena, and the major tributaries of the Río de la Plata. It took much longer to bring North America into cartographic focus. Much was still unexplored, and apparently the De Soto and Coronado expeditions traveled too fast to do much mapping.

In its next phase, Spanish activity in America was turned to the organization and administration of the vast empire won by the conquistadors. The Spaniards wanted to evangelize the millions of Indians, adapt them as far as possible to civilized life, and diffuse as rapidly as possible the Castilian language. These undertakings were accompanied by heavy emigration from Spain; the old charge that the Spaniards failed to colonize is quite without foundation. In Mexico alone, the Spanish population exceeded one million at the beginning of the nineteenth century.

The conquered Indians, dismal as was their fate under the conquest, did not lack Spanish champions. Antonio Montesino, a Dominican living in the West Indies, denounced the ruthless exploitation and decimation of the island population as early as 1511, and secured the passage of a few halfhearted laws to curb the worst excesses. More famous and more effective was another Dominican, Bartolomé de las Casas. This great priest devoted fifty years of his long life to the defense of the Indian victims of Spanish lust and violence. Matching his compatriots' passion for gain and courage under arms with an equal passion for the salvation of human souls and the courage of his Christian convictions, he waged a tireless struggle with soldiers and royal officials to save the Indians from their conquerors. It was he also, more than anyone else, who attempted to preserve the record of the conquest of America, satisfied that the story, if accurately told, would speak for itself. The library he collected for his own use forms the keystone of our knowledge of New World history. Indian rights could not be safeguarded either by the agitation or the writing of Las Casas, but the force of his character and example left an impression that has made him to this day an uncanonized patron saint of the Indian population of Spanish America.

Spain, once the empire had taken shape, governed its economy by the theory of mercantilism, which held that wealth, or at least the most reliable form of wealth, was gold and silver. Since the colonies were supposed to exist for the benefit of the motherland, their principal purpose was to enrich Spain by purchasing her products exclusively and by producing nothing themselves that competed with Spanish goods. In this way, once the loose gold supply of the Aztecs and Incas had been drained off by the conquistadors, Spain expected a constant influx of precious metal from her colonial trade.

The system she erected never functioned well. Although

gold and silver continued to pour across the Atlantic, the trade monopoly could not be wholly maintained, partly because Spain proved unable to supply all the goods her colonists needed, and partly because those she did furnish were sent under such adverse circumstances and were taxed so heavily as to make the prices very high. The colonists evaded the laws when they could, and in the later years of Spain's American regime a large part of their business was done with smugglers.

Mercantilism must not be thought of as a Spanish invention. Most Europeans from the sixteenth through the eighteenth century believed in it, and all the nations building colonial empires during that time tried to put it into practice. But because the Spanish empire was so much larger than the rest, the failure there to enforce mercantilism to the hilt was the most conspicious failure of all.

The story of Spain in America opened with the shattering impact of European civilization on the less-potent civilization of the Indians, but it was not long before the tide of influence turned and Europe began to experience the effects of the great discoveries and conquests across the seas. Gold and silver from Mexico and Peru funneled into the European economy through Spanish ports, vastly increasing the amount of specie in circulation, precipitating a universal rise in prices, and indirectly affecting major political and social developments of the seventeenth century. The introduction of such products as tobacco, chocolate, and potatoes, as well as the vast increase in the production of sugar, rice, cotton, and livestock altered the diet and habits of most Europeans. And while coffee is not an American product by origin, its major entry into Europe was made by way of the New World. It was largely this unlimited expansion of

American agriculture that led to the introduction of Negro slaves. Imported first in small numbers and then by the hundreds of thousands, the colored peoples from Africa became the predominating elements in many parts of the Americas.

With the discovery of the Western Hemisphere, man finally connected the two halves of his world, beyond question the most dramatic and portentous achievement of his recorded efforts. It was Spain that made the first discoveries and the greatest explorations, linking the Old World and the New, and Spain that dominated the exploitation of the New World for a century and more. For these deeds alone the Spanish place in history will be forever secure.

CHAPTER VII

The French Colonial Empire

FRANCE, by contrast with the Iberian countries, was slow in expanding overseas. Portugal lay on the edge of Europe, largely untouched by the crosscurrents of continental strife, and Spain, while less isolated, could pour much of her energy into empire building. But the central position of France caused her embroilment in every major European political or religious feud. When America was discovered, the French king was on the point of armed intervention in the troubled affairs of Italy. This aggressive Italian policy, which he bequeathed to his successors, finally merged into a great struggle with Spain which dragged far into the sixteenth century without a decisive conclusion. Although Spain seemed able to pursue both a European and a colonial policy at the same time, France concentrated on the struggles nearer home, sparing only occasional and spasmodic energies for colonization and exploration overseas.

The Protestant Reformation and ensuing wars of religion consumed French energy for years. Only when Henry IV (1589–1610), the first ruler of the House of Bourbon, came to the throne and stopped the religious struggle could France give serious thought to an overseas empire, and by then many of the best colonial sites had been pre-empted by other powers.

Spasmodic Beginnings

It has been seriously asserted by some French historians that shippers from Normandy explored and traded on the Guinea coast in the fourteenth century years ahead of the Portuguese, and that a French captain, Jean Cousin of Dieppe, discovered the mouth of the Amazon in 1488. But all efforts to verify these legends have come to nothing, and the fact is that patriotic Frenchmen forged evidence of these voyages to give their country a fictitious priority which history denied it.

Still, at the time Spain discovered America and Portugal opened the sea route to India, the French showed some interest in the western and southern Atlantic. Ships of theirs were visiting Brazil soon after 1500 to trade with the natives, to cut the interesting dyewood (*pau brasil*) that gave the country its name, and sometimes to intercept Portuguese spice ships returning from the East. In those early years, when Portugal regarded her great future colony as a worthless land of parrots, reptiles, and cannibals, France appeared likely to claim Brazil for itself. It was largely this dangerous competition that moved the Portuguese government to take the first steps for colonizing Brazil in 1530.

Jean Ango, a shipping proprietor of Dieppe, became the French equivalent of Henry the Navigator. For years he sent out ships, sometimes to seek discoveries but usually to prey on Portuguese vessels in the South Atlantic. In his time the line between legitimate sea enterprise and piracy was hard to draw, and Ango doubtless considered his operations respectable and himself an honorable servant of France. And indeed there was something to be said for him, because he reacted chiefly against the Spanish-Portuguese effort to monopolize the seas. His king, Francis I, complained bitterly against the Treaty of Tordesillas and declared that he would send his ships where he pleased. "I should like to see Adam's will," exclaimed Francis, "wherein he divided the earth between Spain and Portugal."

French Pioneers in America

Though one of Ango's expeditions turned the Cape of Good Hope in 1529 and managed, with the aid of a Portuguese pilot, to reach Sumatra, the French directed most of their early efforts toward America. In 1524 the Italian Giovanni da Verrazano, backed by a group of Frenchmen including Ango, hastily surveyed the North American coast from the Carolinas to Nova Scotia. The purpose of the Verrazano voyage was to find the strait, so much sought by the Spaniards, leading through the American land mass to Marco Polo's Cathay. Since none existed to be found, the next French effort, by Jacques Cartier, naturally was made farther north.

Cartier, a hardy and experienced mariner of St. Malo, though not the first white man to set eyes on Canada, was in every important sense its discoverer. He sailed from France in 1534, being officially in the service of his king in contrast to the earlier private adventurers. On the first voyage he explored the coasts of Newfoundland and Labrador before entering the Gaspé Basin, which he claimed for France. This looked promising as a strait, and so the next year Cartier sailed directly from France to the Gaspé and ascended the

St. Lawrence. He passed up the river to the Indian town of Hochelaga, which he renamed Montreal, and where he found his way blocked by rapids which, significantly, he named Lachine (China). After spending a winter in the St. Lawrence, suffering from scurvy and learning from an Indian of a miraculous juice that effected a cure, Cartier and his men returned to France in 1536. A few years later this captain tried to plant a colony, with the financial support of a gentleman of Picardy, the Sieur de Roberval. Cartier now built a temporary fort on the site of Quebec, but hunger and hardships drove him with his colonists back to France. Roberval tried to hang on a little longer in Canada but soon gave up and went home himself. So far, French colonization efforts had failed miserably.

The next attempt was made in Brazil and but for stupid management might have succeeded. Though the Portuguese had several coastal colonies, their hold on Brazil was still weak and they had overlooked the choicest harbor, Guanabara Bay, the future site of Rio de Janeiro. In 1555 a French soldier named Nicolas Durand de Villegaignon sailed into Guanabara and established a settlement on an island in the bay. His hopes ran high at the moment; he had visions of a great French empire in the south, to be called Antarctic France. But he made the mistake of introducing the religious issue. Thinking, no doubt, to strengthen Antarctic France by an influx of Protestant Huguenots, who were out of favor at home, he wrote John Calvin asking that Protestant theologians be sent to Guanabara. Two Huguenot ministers, accompanied by several laymen, arrived and began preaching their faith to the colonists. Villegaignon, a military man to whom discipline was everything, found this more than he had bargained for, as his own hold on the colony began to slip.

He turned against the Calvinists, everybody took sides, and civil war raged in tiny Antarctic France. Villegaignon, now worried about his future standing at the French court, took ship for home, and the Portuguese quickly put an end to the feeble remnant.

The French Calvinists now tried a colony under their own management. This time they had the backing of the great Huguenot Gaspard de Coligny, Admiral of France. After one abortive attempt, they built a fort in 1564, called Caroline, at the mouth of the St. John's River in northern Florida. They intended, among other things, to use this place as a base for attacking Spanish silver ships homeward bound from Mexico.

Philip II (1556–1598) of Spain could not fail to meet this challenge and sent Menéndez de Avilés to deal with the French heretics. Menéndez, as haughty, bigoted, and brave a Spaniard as ever lived, began by establishing a fort at St. Augustine, a little to the south. Watching his chance, he suddenly fell on the Huguenots, putting all but a few to the sword. Though a few years later one Dominique de Gourgues, an adventurer and slaver from France, destroyed the little post the Spaniards had built on the Fort Caroline site, his act was merely one of revenge. He straightway departed and Spain continued to hold the coast of Florida; St. Augustine survived and is today the oldest city in the United States.

In 1598, when Henry IV of France ended the religious civil wars with the Edict of Nantes, his country was still without American colonies. As the new century opened, however, the French showed signs of entering the colonial arena in earnest.

Serious Efforts in the North

Once more the scene shifted to the north. Around 1600 the French re-explored Acadia (Nova Scotia) and the mouth of the St. Lawrence. Several small and short-lived companies were formed to carry on fur trade with the Indians. The principal consequence of these ventures was the arrival, in 1603, of the famous Samuel de Champlain, who proved to be France's greatest pioneer and explorer. While a French settlement was being made at Port Royal (now named Annapolis) in Acadia, Champlain ascended the St. Lawrence and in 1608 founded Quebec on the old Indian site of Stadacona. A year later he made an alliance with the neighboring Algonquian tribesmen, marched with them against the Iroquois, or Five Nations Confederacy, in central New York, and in a skirmish near the southern end of Lake Champlain defeated one of their war parties. This small engagement had grave historic consequences for France, because the powerful Iroquois, completely alienated, became allies first of the Dutch and then of the English.

Champlain, who lived until 1635, worked hard for the development of Canada, exploring westward to Lake Huron and making many treaties with the Indian tribes. But his Quebec settlement remained poor and struggling. Frenchmen showed little desire to migrate to the New World, and while the fur trade could build a few private fortunes it could not support large numbers. Nor was there gold and silver to attract conquistadors and prospectors in the Spanish-American manner. Though agriculture eventually flourished in the St. Lawrence Valley, many years were required to make it prosper.

The French Jesuits

Even in Champlain's time France made efforts to convert the Indians. A small band of Récolet (Franciscan) friars arrived in Quebec in 1615. Their manpower proved inadequate for the work at hand, and ten years later the main missionary effort was assumed by the Jesuits. The story of the French friars in the heart of North America is an inspiring chapter of courage, adventure, and frequent martyrdom. But compared with the missionary effort in Spanish America the French attempt in the north was not conspicuously successful. This relative failure may be traced to several causes: the smaller numbers, migratory habits, and lower degree of culture of the northern as compared to the southern Indians, the small number of missionaries available to the French, and the general hostility of the French fur traders to the Jesuits. The Spaniards undertook conversion as part of a systematic policy of civilization accompanied by the fostering of agriculture and handicrafts; the French appeared to regard baptism as an end in itself.

Typical of both the heroism and the futility of French missionary labor was the career of Father Isaac Jogues, who after falling prisoner to the Mohawks was taken to their savage abode. There he lived patiently and precariously, subject to every ill treatment at the hands of his brutal hosts, who regarded him as an alien medicine man. He lost no opportunity to splash water on the heads of uncomprehending Mohawk children, whose parents took this for some new species of witchcraft. When at last the tribal leaders decreed his death, Jogues was assisted to escape by kindly Dutch traders at considerable risk to themselves. After a spell of recuperation in France, he returned to the Mohawks and quickly gained the martyr's crown. The Indians remained as heathenish as before.

Cardinal Richelieu

By now the real direction of French policy was in the hands of Cardinal Richelieu, who from 1624 controlled the policies of his king, Louis XIII (1610–1643). A French patriot first and a churchman more or less by accident, Richelieu's main interests always remained European and his chief objective was to weaken the house of Hapsburg, which ruled both Spain and Austria. To do this France must be rich, and getting rich, in Richelieu's mercantilist opinion, meant acquiring a large supply of gold and silver by trade and other means. This program implied the creation of a strong navy, stimulation of French industry and commerce, and acquisition of lucrative colonies.

Richelieu accordingly undertook to do something for Canada, but his interests also turned to the West Indies, where more immediate profit could be expected. By the seventeenth century Spanish sea power was on the decline, and while Spain held the Greater Antilles rather firmly, the Lesser or Outer Antilles remained unoccupied. English merchants and investors had recently begun to push into the Lesser Antilles, followed by a growing stream of immigrants from England. The Dutch, too, had begun to show an interest in the West Indies when France entered the scramble. The main permanent possessions France acquired were the plantation islands of Guadeloupe and Martinique, as well as mainland Cayenne, better known today as French Guiana. Some years after the time of Richelieu, the French grasped the western part of Haiti. Like Guadeloupe and Martinique, this rich plantation colony required a large supply of slaves, and African Negroes were brought in by the thousands.

Whatever his intentions, Richelieu did not accomplish much for Canada. In the year of his death (1642), the permanent French colonists there numbered but a straggling few hundred, perhaps a thirtieth of the number who had already settled in the West Indies. Under Cardinal Mazarin, who succeeded Richelieu and governed France during the long minority of Louis XIV, the population increased at the rate of scarcely a hundred a year.

Policies of Colbert

Jean-Baptiste Colbert, the powerful minister of Louis XIV (1643–1715), dominated French colonial policy from 1661 to 1683. More interested in the economic than in the political side of administration, Colbert was perhaps the greatest mercantilist who ever lived. He found Canada in the hands of trading corporations and was not long in judging that experiment a failure. Colbert therefore transferred the huge territory to royal control, under which it remained until the downfall of France in North America. He stimulated some colonization from France, but most of Canada's slight increase in population was the result of a high birth rate among the settlers, many of whom took Indian wives.

In Colbert's time Canada began to take shape as a colony. Much of the land along the St. Lawrence was divided into feudal grants called seigneuries and distributed among proprietors known as seigneurs. The poor French peasants who worked for the seigneurs were called habitants. This policy of land distribution did not make emigration to Canada look inviting to French peasants, who saw small point in leaving home to become habitants for some Canadian landlord. Furthermore, the policy of forbidding Huguenots to go to

Canada cut off immigrants who later poured eagerly into the rival British settlements and helped them to outstrip the French possession. Therefore, while the white population of Canada grew, it increased so slowly that the colony remained weak and in the eighteenth century proved no match for the faster-growing English to the south.

The French in the West

In the second half of the seventeenth century, the French explored the Mississippi River and the heart of North America. Missionaries such as Fathers Allouez and Marquette, pioneered in the western Great Lakes region. In 1673 Marquette, an indifferent missionary but a better explorer, descended the Mississippi (discovered by De Soto over a hundred years before) in company with a trader, Louis Joliet. The party started under the impression that the Mississippi would prove to be the Colorado River and would empty into the Gulf of California. When they reached the Arkansas country, Marquette and Joliet realized their mistake and turned back.

Next came the famous Robert Cavelier de la Salle, an explorer and fur trader who had a flair for publicizing himself and his projects. La Salle descended the great river from the Illinois country, and on the way smoked the peace pipe and made what he called treaties with various Indian chiefs. Finally, proceeding to the mouth, La Salle took possession of the whole Mississippi Valley in the name of Louis XIV, naming it Louisiana in honor of the king.

La Salle had ambitious plans for a North American empire reaching from the Gulf of Mexico to the Gaspé. Such an empire would have hemmed the English colonies into a small enclave on the Atlantic coast, but for all the advertising La

Salle gave his plan in France it was entirely too ambitious for realization. He intended to make a start by colonizing the mouth of the Mississippi, though when he came from France to the Gulf in charge of a new expedition he missed the river and landed on the coast of Texas. He tried to reach the Illinois country overland, but his high and mighty treatment of his mutinous followers caused them to murder him on the way (1687).

A small part of La Salle's plan was later carried out when the French moved into Louisiana and, in 1718, founded New Orleans. A few posts which they finally built in the Illinois and Indiana country represented a feeble attempt on their part to link Canada closer to Louisiana.

Early in the eighteenth century French traders moved westward and made contact with the Spanish settlements in New Mexico. Farther north other Frenchmen, still ignorant of the mighty mountains that barred the way, sought a path to the Pacific. The Vérendrye brothers came within sight of the Big Horn Mountains west of the Black Hills in 1743 and regretfully abandoned the search for the western sea. Another group of Frenchmen seven years later, approaching by way of the Saskatchewan, was halted by the Rockies themselves. These ventures represented the maximum French advance in North America. Individual achievement had been magnificent, but the net result was insubstantial. The widespread French exploration did little to fortify the French hold, and the mere process of tramping or canoeing over limitless waste areas could be no real substitute for conquest and settlement.

French government in Canada, once the royal agencies had taken control, was arbitrary, paternalistic, and cumbersome. Final authority always remained with the king at

Versailles, whose personal interest in these faraway matters was usually slight. In Canada jurisdiction was divided among local officials by a system of checks and balances which worked to cancel positive action. Under such handicaps initiative faded away and the French colonists, even before their conquest by the English, had begun to lose their loyalty to France.

France in the Old World

In the Old World as well as the New, France expanded. The Senegal country of West Africa had been an important source of slaves ever since its discovery by Prince Henry's Portuguese. In 1626 Richelieu chartered the Normandy Company with a ten-year monopoly of the slave trade. Several quick changes in name and company status followed, but the French kept a foothold in the Senegal. The merchants did not explore the interior very far, but ascended the river annually to barter with the natives for slaves, gold dust, ivory, ostrich feathers, and gum. An attempt in the eighteenth century to extend the French operations to Dahomey failed because of English competition.

In the seventeenth and eighteenth centuries France tried to gain a substantial footing in the great island of Madagascar. After a brief and unsuccessful attempt by French missionaries to work there in the reign of Henry IV, the island coast became an international hangout for pirates, mostly French, Dutch, and English. Though some trade was mixed with piracy, several attempts by French merchants to establish small posts upon the island failed. Even so, France always looked upon Madagascar as her potential property, though before the nineteenth century no successful settlement was made. Meanwhile the French did move into several small near-by islands of the Indian Ocean, principally Île de Bourbon (Réunion) and Mauritius.

It was in India that France ultimately made her main bid for oriental power. By the seventeenth century the Portuguese hold on the Indian Ocean was under attack and weakening fast. Portugal herself had been seized by Philip II in 1580 and virtually annexed to Spain. Though under this new arrangement the Portuguese had the theoretical right to govern and exploit their own colonial empire, the Spanish connection made this empire a natural target for the enemies of Spain. Furthermore, the weakening of Portugal came just at the time when the French, Dutch, and English were ready to build empires of their own.

France had begun to send trading ships around the Cape of Good Hope to India with some regularity as early as 1601. For many years no possessions could be acquired in Hindustan, principally because of the military power of the Mogul emperors, who governed most of the peninsula from their capitals at Delhi and Agra. Under Richelieu and Colbert, attempts were made to extend French trade in the East, accompanied by land explorations across Persia, Asia Minor, and Arabia. French merchants meanwhile secured the right to trade in various Indian cities on the sufferance of the Moguls. Gradually Pondichéry on the east coast became the French headquarters, and the French East India Company, which was in charge of operations, began to assume outright jurisdiction there. After Aurungzeb, the last powerful Mogul emperor, died in 1707, his vast empire commenced to disintegrate, and in the chaos which followed the French found their needed opportunity. From simple trading they passed to politics and constructed a system of alliances and power balances among the petty rulers who had arisen on the ruins of the old empire. Besides Pondichéry, other French posts were developed, such as Chandernagor, Mahé, and Masulipatam.

The English, spearheaded by their own East India Company, were also in India and rivals of the French; but up to about 1750 France seemed to have the upper hand. The French dream of an Indian empire, which came near to being realized under the governorship of Joseph François Dupleix, was dashed forever in the Seven Years' War (1756–1763). Superior English sea power and the genius of Robert Clive, the English East India Company leader, ended all important French influence in Hindustan. The Treaty of Paris (1763) not only expelled France from mainland North America but reduced her to impotence in India. Pondichéry and other posts were retained by the French, but they became in the future insignificant holdings existing by English tolerance.

The Importance of France's Role

In summary, although France came on the colonial scene late, she had an approximately equal start with the Dutch and the English. The French laid the groundwork for a fine empire in North America and India but never proceeded beyond the foundations. Since the reasons for this early French failure have been analyzed many times, only the major points need to be stressed here. In North America, France failed to make immigration desirable to any great number of her people, and as a result the interior of the continent was merely claimed and never held. The ready wealth that came from the West Indies seemed more desirable than the slow, laborious progress to be anticipated from colonization in Canada and Louisiana. French sea power could have become as great as any in Europe, and did flourish for a time under Louis XIV. It was allowed to decay, however, following a naval defeat at English hands in 1692, although, ironically, when the French did build warships their construction was the best in the world. But by neglecting her navy France virtually handed the future to the English, even as her earlier neglect of the sea had worked in favor of the Iberian countries and the Dutch. The great role in continental European politics that France played from the time of Richelieu meant that only in the intervals of peace could the nation attend properly to its colonial affairs. French empire building became a matter of fits and starts; brief spells of energy alternating with periods of neglect. England and the Netherlands, both with less hampering connections on the continent, devoted themselves more wholeheartedly to their territories overseas.

For all that, the part France took in early imperialism was far from insignificant. She bequeathed her language if not her flag to the several million Canadians who are descendants of the seigneurs and habitants of the old regime. Not all the French colonies were lost, and some footholds, such as the one on the Senegal, could be used as bases for expansion in the nineteenth century when the next great wave of imperialism came.

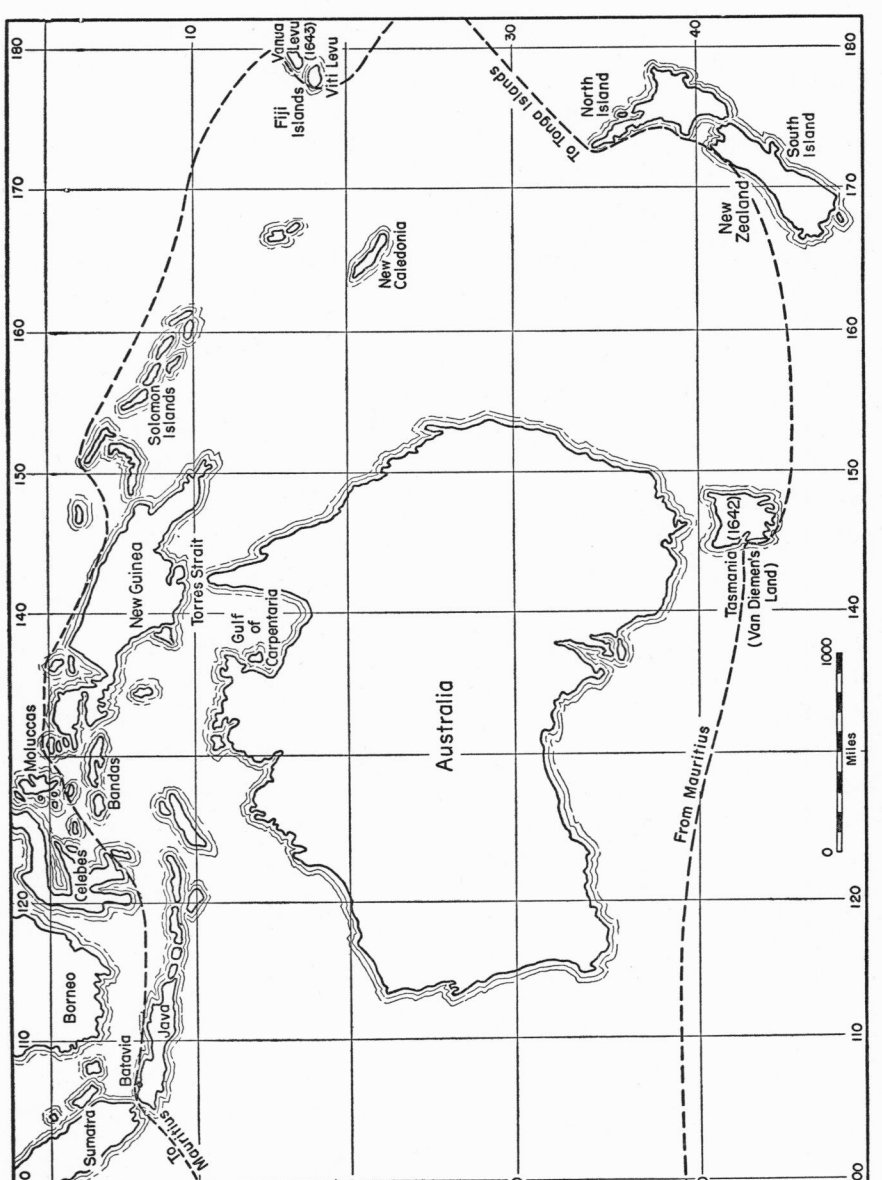

Abel Janszoon Tasman's route around Australia, seventeenth century.

CHAPTER VIII

The Dutch Colonial Empire

THE Dutch Netherlands are a group of eleven provinces of which South and North Holland are by far the richest and most important. During the Middle Ages these lands by the North Sea enjoyed some prosperity but played rather a minor role in European affairs. By the fifteenth and sixteenth centuries, however, their importance had grown. The provinces had developed a common language, essentially the Dutch or *Nederlandsche* spoken today, and showed some signs of developing a national consciousness.

In the fifteenth century the Netherlands fell under the control of the Austrian Hapsburgs, who early in the next century married their way to the Spanish throne. Charles V, who governed so much of Europe, was lord of both Spaniards and Dutchmen; he abdicated, partitioned his empire, and gave Spain and the Netherlands to his son Philip II.

The Dutch thus found themselves, by the process of imperial matrimony, subject to a Spanish king who grew steadily less bearable as time went by. They had considered Charles a tolerable ruler because he spoke their language and frequently lived among them. Philip, on the other hand, was a thoroughgoing Spaniard, speaking only Castilian and seldom leaving Spain. He was by no means the inhuman monster sometimes depicted; it would be truer to say that he was a rather humble man whose stiffness was the result of diffidence. He had, however, an unswerving belief in the rectitude of his own policies and a conscience like that of John Calvin, whose followers he persecuted at every opportunity. Having no temperamental bonds of sympathy with his Dutch subjects, he governed them arbitrarily and with slight attention to local customs and institutions. By this time Protestant doctrines had made a great progress in the Netherlands, and Philip, ever the bulwark of Catholicism, considered the sword and the Inquisition the only means of checking the religious views he hated.

The Dutch rebelled in 1566, and both Catholics and Protestants generally supported the revolution, which gradually became an independence movement. After a confused preliminary period, several of the provinces formed the Union of Utrecht in 1579 and the others eventually adhered to it. The formal declaration of independence came when they substituted an oath of allegiance to the "United Low Countries," for the old one to the king of Spain. After years of bitter warfare, the Dutch began to make headway. Their strongly walled cities could usually resist attack by the famous Spanish infantry, and presently the rebels took to the sea and carried the fight into Spain's home waters. By 1595, the war for independence, though still dragging on, seemed as good as won. Spain made several later efforts at reconquest, however, and the fight raged at intervals until the Treaty of Westphalia in 1648 formally recognized the independence of the provinces.

The sea phase of the Dutch revolt ushered in the great colonial empire of the Netherlands. Already the provinces had a large merchant marine, which traded from the Baltic to Guinea. In 1580 Philip II had seized Portugal, following the death of a childless Portuguese king. For some years he did not try to stop the thriving trade that went on between Lisbon and his rebellious Dutch subjects. Then, thinking to deal the Netherlanders a crippling economic blow, he passed a series of embargoes closing the Tagus River to their ships. This cut the Dutch out of any share of the spices that the Portuguese still brought back from the East. It also deprived them of their main supply of salt, which they had bought in Portugal and which they needed to cure their large catches of fish from the North Sea.

Dutch Arctic Exploration

The Spanish embargo on Dutch-Portuguese trade backfired on Philip. The Netherlanders decided to cut loose from their European moorings and go to the East Indies for spices and the West Indies for salt. Of the two, the eastern islands had the greater interest for them. But they wished to do more than merely follow the Portuguese path to the East, they set out to see if other routes could be found. First they tried the northeast, an idea that the English had entertained and abandoned years before. Seeking the Northeast Passage meant sailing north of Scandinavia and groping along the Russian and Siberian coasts for a way to the Pacific. Only ignorance of the geographical difficulties involved gave early explorers the courage to try. It was not until 1878–1879 that the Swedish explorer, Baron A. E. Nordenskiöld, finally made this voyage, in the *Vega*. Beginning in 1594 the Dutch made three such attempts, their main achievements being the rediscovery of bleak Nova Zemlya and Spitsbergen, where they suffered severely before returning home. This made the northern prospect look rather forlorn, but the Dutchmen did not quite lose hope.

In 1609 the Dutch East India Company hired the Englishman Henry Hudson, who had already sailed in Arctic waters, to try the northeast again. Hudson, in his famous little *Half Moon,* obediently started in the Nova Zemlya direction but soon decided that this quest would come to nothing. So he crossed the Atlantic and looked for the Northwest Passage instead. He found the bay of New York and the Hudson River, up which the *Half Moon* sailed as far as the site of Albany, and narrowly missed encountering Champlain, who was exploring near by. Since Hudson had made the voyage in Dutch service, his "discovery," though lacking originality by 1609, gave the Netherlands a claim to the region, which they later tried to colonize.

The Dutch in the Far East

Many Dutch seamen in the past had shipped aboard Portuguese fleets for India and some had returned to tell what they had learned. Especially important was the experience of Jan Huyghen van Linschoten, who sailed from Lisbon to Goa and who, once back in Europe, published an account of the route with full details. Utilizing his information, Cornelis de Houtman, commanding four Dutch ships, braved the Cape of Good Hope and the Indian Ocean in 1595 to reach Java. The three vessels that returned bore very slim cargoes, but the voyage, if no financial success, showed that Dutchmen, as well as Portuguese, could make the trip and return.

Optimism flourished to such an extent that in 1598 twenty-two ships put out of the Zuider Zee for the East Indies. Since the Netherlanders had no part in the old

Spanish-Portuguese Treaty of Tordesillas, they were free
to try both main routes to the East. Thirteen of their vessels
turned the Cape of Good Hope, while the other nine elected
to go through the Strait of Magellan. The bulk of the main
contingent returned richly laden with pepper and nutmeg,
but only one member of the Strait of Magellan group
reached home. This lone ship, commanded by Olivier van
Noort, escaped through the Indian Ocean after many hair-
raising adventures with the Spaniards in the Philippines, to
complete the first Dutch voyage around the world.

The Dutch East India Company

In 1602 the Netherlanders founded their highly capitalized
United East India Company. Though a private concern, this
corporation had a close connection with the Dutch government, now an aristocratic body of legislators known as the
States-General. The Company received a monopoly of all
Dutch trade east of the Cape of Good Hope and west of
the Strait of Magellan—in other words a free hand in the
Indian and Pacific Oceans. Though not planned as an
empire-building agency, it had power to carry on war with
the Spaniards and the Portuguese and could also conduct
negotiations with oriental princes. It fast gained the upper
hand in the eastern islands, driving the Portuguese out of
Amboina and dealing mercilessly with Englishmen who attempted to move in.

Jan Pieterszoon Coen was the real architect of the Dutch
oriental empire. The city of Batavia, in Java, which he
founded, became the eastern headquarters for the Company
and dominated the whole trade of the Far East. Coen put
down all resistance by the Javanese princes, conquered the
Banda Islands, and replaced the Portuguese trade mastery of

the Moluccas with a Dutch one. When he died in 1629, there was no doubt about Netherlands control of the East Indies. Coen was one of the first Europeans to recognize the value of Japanese soldiers. He preferred them to any others as mercenaries and maintained that none could surpass them in bravery, though it is safe to say that he never foresaw the time, three centuries later, when they would take from the Dutch that very empire he had labored to build.

The Dutch, like the Portuguese before them, presently learned that oriental empires cost too much to be solely a matter of collecting profits. Some years the Company paid handsome dividends to the stockholders at home; at other times it had no gains to show. Often it produced spectacular military results or geographical knowledge, which investors considered a poor substitute for financial rewards.

Cape Horn

The Netherlanders now regularly used the Strait of Magellan as well as the Cape of Good Hope to reach the Indies, even though there was some danger from the Spaniards, whose power in South America and on the sea was still great. Cape Horn lies far south of the strait and forms the tip of an island below Tierra del Fuego. No one had yet discovered the cape, though Francis Drake had been somewhat south of it in 1578 during his voyage around the world. According to a European theory, which Drake had not dispelled, no such thing as Cape Horn could exist. Tierra del Fuego was thought to be a peninsula stretching up from a giant continent in the south, commonly called *Terra Australis*, much vaster than the Antarctic Continent that later was found. It was the Dutch who revealed that Tierra del Fuego was no part of a continent, but an island with open water to the south.

Their discovery of Cape Horn grew out of a free-lance effort to break a monopoly. The States-General of the Netherlands had already given the East India Company the sole right to trade in the Orient by way of the Cape of Good Hope and the Strait of Magellan, thus cutting private merchants out of any share of eastern commerce. This, however, did not prevent many of them from wanting a part of it; and Isaac Le Maire, one of the malcontents, reasoned that if a new way could be found to enter the Pacific there would be no violation of the company's privileges. With this in mind he formed his own little company, with capital raised mostly in the town of Hoorn by the Zuider Zee, and sent out two ships. The commander, Willem Schouten, boldly sailed past the entrance to the Strait of Magellan, and in January 1616 he rounded the promontory ". . . whereat we were very glad, holding that a way had been discovered by us which had until then been unknown to man. . . . It consisted entirely of high mountains covered with snow, and ends in a sharp corner, which we called the Cape of Hoorn, and which lies in latitude 57° 48'S." This was an error; it is really in 55° 59'S. The discoverers then made their way across the Pacific, but on reaching the East Indies fell into the hands of that jealous watchdog of the company's monopoly, Coen. He contemptuously rejected their nonsense about finding a new cape and accused them of trespass and violation of company rights. Schouten's one remaining ship was confiscated and the commander was sent home to stand trial in the Netherlands. Luckily for Schouten, his patron, Le Maire, proved a stout legal fighter who won the case and compelled the company to hand back the ship and pay damages. The Cape Horn route now became an important factor in navigation, though many thought that it was merely another strait and that the great southern continent lay not far south.

Abel Tasman

An equally famous exploration was that of Australasia by Abel Janszoon Tasman some years later. Spanish and Portuguese voyagers had stumbled on parts of the Australian coast, and in the early seventeenth century a few Dutch ships had found land in the vicinity of Torres Strait and the Gulf of Carpentaria. But beyond the knowledge that some land lay there, the picture was very vague.

In 1642 Anthony van Diemen was governor of the Dutch East Indies. This energetic man, the ablest of Coen's successor's, did not feel sure that all sources of Pacific trade had been found and so began explorations in several directions. To the north his ships went as far as the Kuril Islands beyond Japan. To investigate southward, Van Diemen selected the seasoned Captain Tasman and ordered him to explore the great land, already several times reported, with an eye to its commercial possibilities and any treasure it might contain. Tasman sailed from Batavia and first struck westward in the Indian Ocean to Mauritius, where a small Dutch settlement existed. Returning toward the east, he passed below Australia, missing the continent entirely and discovering Tasmania, which he named Van Diemen's Land. He could not be sure whether Tasmania was a separate island or part of the larger land mass, though he guessed it to be a peninsula of Australia. A theory among his men to the effect that the unseen inhabitants were giants prevented much land exploration from being done. Sailing still farther eastward, Tasman found the two lands which he named New Zeeland (Zealand) after the Netherlands province. Again he could not be certain that these were islands, because he saw only their western coasts, and believed they might be parts of some larger mass. Passing northward, Tasman concluded his discoveries by finding both the Tonga and Fiji Islands before he returned to Batavia by way of New Guinea.

By sailing around the real Australia, Tasman had proved that it could not be part of the theoretical *Terra Australis*, with which European imaginations filled so much of the South Pacific. But he did not eliminate this mythical continent from future geographical calculation, for by finding the two New Zealand islands he raised the speculation that they were part of *Terra Australis*. Unfortunately no Dutch explorers followed Tasman to those regions, since the company chose not to waste ships and money on discoveries that seemed to promise no economic return. So *Terra Australis*, as distinct from the actual Australia and the Antarctic continent, lived on in men's imaginations for another hundred years and more, until the voyages of Captain Cook proved that it could not possibly exist.

The Dutch West India Company

Though the States-General had given to the monopolistic East India Company the Pacific and Indian Oceans, they did not award any rights in the Atlantic until 1621, when they established the Dutch West India Company. The new corporation received a trade monopoly and colonization rights in the New World and along the west African coast south of the Tropic of Cancer.

The West India Company was launched just at the moment when war with the king of Spain had been resumed.

Not having much capital, the new company meant to operate largely as a privateering enterprise, to enrich itself with spoils from Spanish and Portuguese ships, and to gain control of the profitable slave trade.

One of the early acts of the directors was to take over jurisdiction of the Hudson River. A few straggling Dutch settlers already lived scattered through this area, and the company assumed control of them. It sent out a few more, built Fort Amsterdam, and made the renowned twenty-four-dollar purchase of Manhattan Island from the Indians. With better management this Dutch venture could have grown. But the company directors and the settlers had little in common, and the history of their mutual relations is a story of incessant quarreling. The governors sent out were generally inept and always unpopular. The last of them, peppery, wooden-legged Petrus Stuyvesant, let the citizens know that if any man appealed over his jurisdiction to the home authorities he would "make him a foot shorter, and send the pieces home to Holland, and let him appeal that way." The system of patroon grants, which gave much of the best land on the lower Hudson to Dutch capitalists— Van Cortlandts, Van Rensselaers, and Schuylers—tended to keep immigrants away. Fur trade with the Indians, which was the ostensible reason for the colony's existence, proceeded very slowly. The settlers showed an occasional burst of energy against the English in Connecticut and the Swedes on the Delaware, but neither they nor the directors at home expressed much regret when England took over the colony in 1664.

From first to last the West India Company poured most of its men and money into Brazil and adjacent regions of the South Atlantic. The great plan of capturing the slave trade meant securing both ends of the traffic: the supply in Guinea and Angola and the market in Portuguese Brazil. Sugar raising, which was the principal purpose of all this slavery, had by now become a giant factor in world economy.

In 1624 the Dutch captured Baía in Brazil, but lost the place almost at once. This costly failure cut deep into the company treasury, but a stroke of luck followed when Admiral Piet Pieterszoon Heyn took a Spanish silver fleet off Matanzas in Cuba. Encouraged and refinanced, the Dutch attacked Brazil again, this time capturing Olinda near Recife. They followed up their success by taking St. Eustatius and Curaçao in the West Indies. Within a few years further operations in Brazil brought the whole coast from Recife to the mouth of the Amazon into Dutch hands.

The company's governor in Brazil, the able Johan Maurits of Nassau-Siegen, was by disposition an empire builder who scorned such vulgar matters as financial reckonings. It may not be quite fair to say, as some do, that his plans failed only because of the penny-pinching of the directors at home; the whole adventure was certainly too ambitious for the resources of the company. Unquestionably, however, there was disagreement between the aristocratic Johan Maurits and the profit-hungry, bourgeois directors whose parsimony or poverty caused him to return home disgruntled in 1644. Even so, he remained in control long enough to start the other phase of the expansion program, the capture of Portuguese Angola in West Africa. The Dutch took São Paulo de Luanda, the main Angolan seaport, and seemed to have a bright future in the slave trade.

But now the tide turned. The Portuguese still held southern Brazil, and their morale was decidedly raised when their mother country revolted from Spain in 1640 and regained its independence. After the retirement of Johan Maurits, the Portuguese took the offensive and recovered their Brazilian colonies one by one, along with São Paulo de Luanda and a few South Atlantic islands that the Dutch had recently seized from them.

The West India Company's South Atlantic empire thus collapsed as fast as it had risen. When New Netherland was lost in 1664, the Dutch found themselves without a single holding in continental America. In the West Indies they had only Curaçao and a few minor islands. Though a little later they managed to get Surinam, better known today as Dutch Guiana, this was poor compensation for what they had grasped and lost.

Dutch failure in the Atlantic, contrasted with Dutch success in the Orient, suggests that the West India Company directors did not manage as well as did their countrymen who controlled the East. It is easy today, by the use of hindsight, to discover all their mistakes. The company indeed neglected the Hudson Valley, while squandering Dutch resources in a well-nigh hopeless effort to take Brazil. But scarcely anyone in the seventeenth century saw that this was a mistake; even England attached more value to the tropics than to North America. If the slave trade proved a tempting bait to the Dutch directors, it furnished the same temptation to other Europeans. The real criticism to be leveled at the Dutch policy is that the slave trade was too large a business and altogether too competitive for one nation, let alone one corporation, to monopolize.

Certainly a major cause of the company's failure was the initial decision to make the whole enterprise a predatory one. Spanish and Portuguese plunder alone could not keep the treasury full. Sending marauding ships to sea was expensive, and every one returning empty represented a dead loss. Though Heyn brought home a sum reported as 11,000,000 guilders when he took the Spanish plate fleet off Cuba, this great success was never repeated. The Spaniards and Portuguese improved their defensive measures and furthermore knew how to play the plundering game themselves.

South Africa

South Africa cannot be overlooked in surveying the colonial achievements of the Dutch. The Portuguese, in their heyday, had neglected the most important station on the India route, the Cape of Good Hope itself. The Dutch also neglected it until one of their ships was wrecked in Table Bay just north of the Cape on the Atlantic side. The crew survived and lived on friendly terms with the natives, growing their own food and carrying on a little trade. When these men were picked up, their story interested the directors of the East India Company. Acting on company orders, Jan van Riebeeck dropped anchor in the bay in 1652 with the purpose of founding a colony and pitched camp off the present site of Capetown.

Riebeeck, who had lived in the East, wished to settle the cape with Chinese, knowing them to be the cheapest colonists that could be had. When the authorities in Batavia refused to send him a coolie supply, he built his settlement with slaves and a handful of Dutch. Once founded, Capetown soon proved its value. East India Company ships, bound to and from the Orient, put in there to obtain supplies of fresh meat and vegetables. This helped keep down scurvy, which was a menace on any long voyage, and saved the lives of thousands of seamen. Not only did the Dutch profit from their handy way station; other Europeans sailing around the cape soon were doing so as well. The Dutchmen, along with some French Huguenots, who colonized the southern end of Africa became the ancestors of the present-day Afrikanders or Boers.

The Far East Again

In the Orient, the Dutch more than held their own. By 1641 the old Portuguese stronghold of Malacca had been captured and the Netherlanders had a firm foothold on the important strait. Later they pushed north to Macassar, while at the same time they increased the size of their possessions in Java and Sumatra. They ultimately drove the Portuguese from Ceylon and for a while held part of Formosa. The trading contact that they established with Japan remained the only European connection with the island empire until Commodore Perry ended Japanese isolation in the middle of the nineteenth century. Soon after 1700 the nature of the East India Company's economic activity changed somewhat with the introduction of coffee culture into Java from Arabia. Stimulated by a growing consumption in Europe, where coffeehouses for a time threatened to outstrip taverns in popularity, the berry rapidly became a major export of the East Indies.

Decline of Dutch Power

By the end of the seventeenth century the Netherlands were on the way to becoming a secondary power. A country so small was in the long run unequal to the task of competing with great nations like England and France. The Dutch had borne the brunt of the attack against the old monopolists, Spain and Portugal, and they above all others had brought low the mighty power of Spain. But when the Hollanders attempted to continue the struggle for world mastery against both England and France, the wars with these countries pared down the magnificent navy and merchant marine that in the middle of the century had been the greatest in the world. For carrying on ocean trade the Dutch geographical position proved inferior to that of the English. England lay directly athwart the Dutch sea path, and when the two countries fought, British control of the channel and the waters north of Scotland forced the ships from the Zuider Zee to run an unpleasant gauntlet.

Other causes of decline, less easy to weigh and measure, were also present. There seems to have been some deterioration in Dutch leadership as the century progressed. For a while the Netherlanders, by their superior business methods, navigational skill, and technical dexterity in the lading and handling of ships, became the leaders and envy of all Europe. The old phrase "to beat the Dutch" reflects the onetime ambition of the English to rival or surpass their neighbors across the North Sea. When ultimately they did beat the Dutch, the latter could never regain the lead they had lost. Most important of all, however, seems to have been the slow process of attrition, which just as in Portugal's case a century before, took its yearly toll of a small nation attempting the work of a large one. The Netherlands played their last great power role in the War of the Spanish Succession (1701–1713), after which they seemed glad to subside to a secondary position.

The Dutch colonial empire was more economic and secular than were any of the others. All nations thought of colonies as fields of exploitation and sources of profit. But Spain, Portugal, and France felt the need to spread religion, and did so with varying degrees of success. Several of the

English colonies had a strongly religious basis. With the Dutch, strong Calvinists though they were at home, the zeal for conversion seemed lacking. Company directors had small interest in the souls of the natives who raised their cloves, nutmegs, and coffee berries. Those ministers of the Dutch Reformed Church who went to the colonies worked among their own people and left the East Indians and American Indians alone.

But if the Dutch had little missionary zeal they had great scientific curiosity. Of all colonial nations they learned most about the flora, fauna, and other natural features of their empire. During the seventeenth and eighteenth centuries their scholars were easily the leaders in geography, cartography, and oceanography.

This all illustrates the fact that the Dutch colonial empire was a business proposition. The home country has been likened to a large-scale trading corporation with the States-General as the board of directors. The comparison is a good one, even though in other lines the Dutch were proving themselves far more than mere materialists. The century that produced the East and West India Companies also produced Rembrandt, Vermeer, and Frans Hals. For all that, the typical Hollander of the seventeenth century was the stockholder and the merchant prince.

CHAPTER IX

The First English Colonial Empire

WHEN Columbus discovered America, England was slowly recovering from a series of national misfortunes. The Hundred Years' War with France, after putting a great strain on the country, had ended in disaster, only to be followed by the even more futile Wars of the Roses, in which the partisans of Lancaster and York slaughtered each other at home. When Henry VII (1485–1509) of the house of Tudor grasped the throne in 1485, he put an end to civil war, but many problems remained. Throughout his reign Henry worked tirelessly to build up an efficient absolutism and to replenish the treasury; strict economy had to be his watchword and he was in no position to waste much in adventures across the ocean.

England at the start of the Tudor era lay near the outer rim of the known world. Only Iceland, poor and backward, existed to the northwest, and nothing was known beyond Ireland to the west. The English had yet to build their seafaring reputation; their merchant marine was small and most of their trade was carried in foreign bottoms. Some native shipping plied between Bristol and Ireland, bringing home fish in exchange for wool and salt. But the Venetian galleys still made their annual voyages to England, and from across the North Sea came the trading vessels of the Hanseatic League.

Records show, however, that a few Bristol merchants had plans for exploring the Atlantic by 1480, when one of them sent a ship to look for the legendary island of Brazil, commonly thought to lie west of Ireland. We likewise know that a few years later Bartholomew Columbus tried to interest Henry VII in his brother's discovery plan. Though Bartholomew got a courteous hearing, nothing came of it, and not until John Cabot's voyage did England's government show a real interest in the western ocean.

The Cabot Voyages

Cabot was an Italian, born Giovanni Caboto in Genoa or some town near by. He was both a merchant and a skilled navigator and had once traveled eastward beyond Suez. By 1491 he had settled in Bristol, whose merchants are known, from evidence recently found, to have already discovered Newfoundland. In all probability, Cabot himself had thought of a voyage to the land of eastern luxuries.

By 1496 Bristol traders had made a partner of Cabot, whose knowledge of oriental trade they needed, and their joint decision was to use Newfoundland, which they called "Brasil," as the first step toward trading ventures with Cipangu and Cathay, believed to lie farther south. King Henry invested no money in the voyage but did issue a patent giving the Italian the right to sail to any part of the world unknown to Christians.

The Bristol investors planned a good-sized expedition, but as their preparations took time, Cabot decided to make a cheap voyage of reconnaissance ahead of the main party. On May 2, 1497, he left Bristol in the little ship *Matthew*. With a crew of eighteen men which included his son Sebastian, he crossed the Atlantic west of Ireland and probably sighted the New World around Cape Breton Island. The *Matthew*, according to a perhaps exaggerated report, coasted the American mainland for about 300 leagues, seeing no inhabitants but noting various signs of their existence. In exactly fifty-four days Cabot was back in Bristol. His return created a minor sensation, and the captain went up to London, where Henry VII, with characteristic frugality, gave him a royal welcome and a reward of ten pounds.

The next year Cabot sailed in command of the main expedition. Since the discoverers thought they were bound for the vicinity of Marco Polo's Cathay, their disillusionment with what they found can be easily understood. Nothing is known of the adventure beyond the fact that more coast was explored; and some have thought that Cabot lost his life in the voyage. More likely, however, the failure to find wealth and open trade finished his career; the next Cabot achievements were those of his son Sebastian.

Until near the end of Henry's reign there is little trace of further English voyages to America. The king, for family reasons, had every wish to keep on good terms with Spain; yet though he would not poach on Spanish discoveries he evidently saw no harm in exploring to the far north. Sebastian Cabot appears to have sailed up the Labrador coast in 1509 and to have found the entrance to Hudson's Bay; reaching 67° N. before the cold drove him back. He was obviously seeking a northwest passage to Cathay, since his father's voyages had shown that North America was not the region Marco Polo had visited and that to reach Cathay the new land must somehow be rounded. But Sebastian returned to England to find the king dead and the throne now occupied by Henry VIII (1509–1547), who showed no interest in Arctic exploration. English service now had nothing for Sebastian Cabot, who with royal permission accepted an offer from Ferdinand of Spain. He won fame in Spanish employment, and became the third holder of the pilot major's office, previously filled by Vespucci and Solís.

English Maritime Progress

Henry VIII, that much-married monarch who engineered the English break from the Roman Church, paid no particular attention to discovery. During his thirty-eight-year reign, nevertheless, the Royal Navy expanded from an original seven ships to fifty-three and at the same time largely abandoned the outmoded galley in favor of sailing vessels. Great improvements came in seamanship, artillery, and gunnery. The pride of the navy was the newly built *Henry Grace à Dieu,* a four-masted ship of about 1,000 tons, bristling with guns and equipped with the latest type of sails. English warships gave good performances in battles up and down the channel with the French. Thus while Henry's England failed to shine in exploration, its interest in the sea increased, in fortunate anticipation of a day when national salvation would depend on nautical prowess.

In 1548, the year following Henry's death, Sebastian Cabot returned to England, still full of his youthful hope of finding a northern route to the East. Five years later he planned his last expedition, whose purpose was to find a northeast passage. He organized an association of English merchants interested in the new route he offered to Cathay. Cabot, now past seventy, was judged too old to sail, and when he defiantly demonstrated his vigor by performing a dance on deck just before the ships' departure, he drew applause but no reversal of that decision. Sir Hugh Willoughby commanded the vessels, with Richard Chancellor as his subordinate. After the fleet had been separated by storms, Willoughby discovered Nova Zemlya, only to die in Lapland; Chancellor, with better luck, entered the White Sea and made his way to Moscow. Tsar Ivan the Terrible not only welcomed the Englishman graciously but sent him home with a letter suggesting that trade be started between their two countries. The original backers of the voyage now formed the Muscovy Company and sent as their agent to Moscow Anthony Jenkinson, who made another futile attempt to sail past the White Sea. Convinced that the Northeast Passage was out of the question and deciding to try a new way to the East, Jenkinson traveled by land across Russia to Bokara and managed to open a short-lived trade with Persia.

The Merchants Adventurers

The Muscovy Company was only one of several trading enterprises started in Tudor England. The Eastland Company was created for trade with Poland and the Baltic; the Levant Company for commerce with the eastern Mediterranean and Turkey. Finally, in 1600, shortly before the death of Queen Elizabeth, there came into existence the English East India Company, which in time was to prepare the way for another British queen to become Empress of India.

A natural assumption might be that these trading enterprises created wealth in England by tapping new sources of commerce. But the facts fail to bear out the assumption. Since the companies all existed for private profit and thought of nothing but their own gain, they tried always to organize monopolies that froze trade and killed off competition. The merchants adventurers, as these overseas traders were called, proved no unmixed blessing.

English Arctic Exploration

During the forty-five year reign of Elizabeth (1558–1603), England became a power on the sea. The thrilling adventures of her sea dogs will always be remembered with pride by the English, but their deeds have been described so often elsewhere that only the briefest summary need be attempted here.

From 1576 to 1578 Martin Frobisher made three voyages to the vicinity of Labrador and Greenland in search of the northwest passage. Fondly believing that he had struck gold in southern Baffin Land, Frobisher brought home for assay a shipload of worthless dirt, which for decades was piled just inside the gate of the Tower of London to block traffic in and out. A colonial plan of his also fell through, and this gallant but unlucky explorer was forced to stop from lack of funds.

John Davis, following Frobisher to the north, gave western Greenland a more thorough exploration and discovered Davis Strait, up which he sailed to latitude 72° N. before being pounded back by a gale. A few years after Elizabeth's death, Henry Hudson, now back in English service, entered the great bay which bears his name and which Sebastian Cabot may have penetrated a century earlier. Hudson's career ended here, for his crew mutinied and set him adrift in a small boat. He was never seen again. It was left for William Baffin, who voyaged in 1615, to prove that, contrary to English bright hopes, Hudson Bay was not the coveted Northwest Passage. Having verified the discouraging fact, Baffin pressed still further north to enter and chart Baffin Bay. This seemed to promise nothing, and following his return Englishmen for many years abandoned the search for the passage. Only in the twentieth century did the Norwegian, Roald Amundsen, in his stout little *Gjoa*, finally make the northwest voyage the old mariners had so long and painfully attempted.

Elizabethan Sea Dogs

Although the queen began her reign at peace with Spain, the religious issue and European politics led Elizabeth and Philip II to an estrangement that widened until undeclared war raged between them. The English at first made some effort to trade peacefully with Spanish America. John Hawkins came to grief when he tried to open slave trade between the Guinea coast and the Caribbean colonies of Spain. He was caught with six ships at Vera Cruz by a Spanish armada, which opened fire without warning. After Hawkins had limped back to England with a crippled remnant of his fleet, war was open and bitter between Spaniards and Englishmen in the New World, whatever lip service their rulers paid to peace in Europe.

The greatest sea dog of all was Francis Drake. Being one of the survivors of the Hawkins debacle at Vera Cruz, he burned for revenge and repeatedly exacted it in blood and treasure. After harassing the Spaniards in the West Indies, he broke into the Pacific through Magellan's Strait, and raided the coasts of Chile and Peru. Next, seeking the Strait of Anian, he passed northward to some point on the California coast, which he claimed for his queen and called New Albion. He left a brass plate near San Francisco Bay as witness to the claim, and in 1936 a picnic party from Oakland found a brass plate which answers to the description of

Drake's. Crossing the Pacific to the East Indies and sailing on through the Indian Ocean, he returned to England in 1580 loaded with plunder. As the first Englishman to circumnavigate the globe, Drake was given a most gracious welcome by Elizabeth, his queen, who shared generously in the loot. This exploit stimulated another English commander, Thomas Cavendish, to enter the Pacific, play havoc with the Spaniards, cross the great ocean, and round the globe. Meanwhile, Drake and others redoubled their attacks on Spanish shipping in the Atlantic and the West Indies.

The Armada

Philip II, by 1587, had stood all he meant to endure from England. Slowly he began to collect his naval power in Atlantic ports to carry his armies across from the Netherlands to invade the hated island. The English had ample warning, and Sir Francis Drake, whom the queen had knighted for his famous voyage, delayed the attack somewhat by managing to destroy several of the best Spanish ships by a surprise attack at Cadiz. But "singeing the King of Spain's beard," as Drake himself described it, did not stop the preparations, and in 1588 the armada sailed.

The outcome is known to all. Philip's fleet, consisting of about 120 big ships, undermanned, ill-equipped, weak in fire power, and badly commanded, was attacked in the channel by the now expert English seamen and gunners and, if not destroyed, was at least driven past the appointed place of rendezvous with the Spanish Netherlands army and into the North Sea, where bitter winds compelled the ill-starred armada to sail completely around the British Isles in a cruise that cost further ships and men in the unfamiliar and treacherous waters off Scotland and Ireland. Less than half of the fleet returned to Spain.

Historians have tended to exaggerate the material effects of Spain's defeat. It by no means ended Philip's sea power, and the bitter lessons the Spaniards learned actually brought improvement in their ships and tactics. The English had been in less danger, probably, than they believed at the time; even had the plan of Philip worked to perfection it is doubtful whether his Netherlands army could have conquered or long held any large part of England. Still, the whole episode was wrapped in drama, and we cannot overlook the great uplift in English morale that came as a result of this triumph over the master of half the earth.

English Colonization

It is also an exaggeration to say that the sea dogs, by attacking Spain, cleared the way for later English colonization. Operating from an England which possessed limited capital and manpower, the seadogs directed most of their efforts toward get-rich-quick schemes involving either Spanish plunder or the discovery of gold. Sea dogging ate up capital, and every pound or shilling that went into this semipiracy was a pound or shilling taken away from something else. A few voyages, such as Drake's, paid handsomely, but the average showed a loss. It is reasonable to assume, therefore, that the resources spent, and largely wasted, on plundering expeditions might have given England a solid foothold in America before Elizabeth's death. As it was, the English had yet to plant a successful colony when the new century began.

Three small efforts had already been made. Sir Humphrey

Gilbert had tried to settle Newfoundland in 1582, and a little later Sir Walter Raleigh had twice made similar attempts at Roanoke. The endeavors all failed, and the mystery of the total disappearance of Raleigh's second colony, numbering over a hundred, is still unsolved. Since the Indians living in the vicinity were warlike, a reasonable guess can be made as to the fate of these unfortunate people, but the problem still intrigues students of American history.

Gilbert and Raleigh had not worked in vain, and at the turn of the century the cause found a champion in Richard Hakluyt. A lifelong student of geography and a tireless collector of the earlier great narratives of discovery, as well as a member of the Virginia Company, he offered able and learned arguments for colonies. Far more contagious than his learning was his enthusiasm, which entitles him to be called the intellectual progenitor of the British Empire. Francis Bacon, too, although less enthusiastic than Hakluyt, wrote sagely on the subject of colonization, and his essay *Of Plantations* remains a classic. Pamphleteers, many of them anonymous, contributed opinions regarding colonies and their management which if not always expert were at least confidently expressed. And behind the theories lay the backlog of experience provided by sundry English attempts to settle the wastes of Ireland.

Virginia and Plymouth

The first permanent overseas English colony was founded on the James River in 1607 by the Virginia Company of London, whose managers believed gold could be found near Chesapeake Bay. For the first few years the colony seemed sure to fail, as disease, laziness, inability to raise food, and

Indian trouble almost wrecked the enterprise. At this crucial time the energy of Captain John Smith, whose colorful career had already taken him, as he declared, from Turkey to Morocco, proved decisive in saving the colony. More important than the adventure with Pocahontas, which has been doubted but never disproved, were his Indian diplomacy, his successful efforts to secure food, and his ability to manage the shiftless and dispirited colonists. Smith did not long remain in Virginia, but able governors took charge; and within a few years tobacco had been introduced as the staple crop, the colony had moved from the original Jamestown to a better site, and self-governing institutions had been started. Meanwhile, a branch of the Virginia Company began the settlement of the Bermudas, whose colonists soon threatened to outstrip the mainlanders as tobacco producers.

Captain John Smith continued to be a staunch advocate of colonization after his return to England. Somewhat later he became interested in fisheries north of Virginia and mapped a stretch of coast which he called New England. In 1620 a little party of English religious dissenters, some of whom had lived in the tolerant Netherlands, crossed the Atlantic in the *Mayflower*. Partly perhaps on the strength of Smith's favorable New England propaganda, these colonists settled at Plymouth. The Pilgrim Fathers, to be quite frank, have a greater place in American lore than in American history. Their colony began small and remained small, to be soon overshadowed and finally annexed by its powerful neighbor, Massachusetts Bay. Yet as long as Thanksgiving remains an American holiday and as long as Myles Standish, John Alden, and Priscilla Mullens are remembered, the fame of this tiny settlement will live.

The Puritan Movement

On Elizabeth's death, the English throne had passed to James I (1603–1625) of the Scottish house of Stuart. James was an opinionated man of some learning; "the wisest fool in Christendom," as one of his contemporaries declared. Coming to London from poverty-stricken Scotland, he expected to reign in opulence, but found the absolutism of his Tudor predecessors impossible to maintain. Everything, including government, now cost more, partly because of the great amount of gold and silver Spain had poured into Europe from America. With the menace of Spanish conquest now gone, Parliament and the moneyed classes demanded reforms in government and in taxes. James had religious troubles as well. The Church of England, established in Tudor times, was already splitting badly. The Puritan faction had grown strong enough to demand that the Established Church be purged of bishops and all Roman forms and symbols. The Puritans were Calvinists in creed, being close in that respect to the Presbyterians, who had already gained the dominance in King James's original home, Scotland. They did not, however, mean to leave the Church of England; they intended instead to remain in it and, by securing control, to "purify" it. Even those who ultimately moved to America postponed a formal secession for many years. The Puritans differed in this respect from the Pilgrim settlers of Plymouth; the Pilgrims, holding rigid Calvinist doctrines, had seceded bag and baggage from the Established Church and had gone to America as independents.

Parliament was swinging toward Puritanism, for the movement counted among its followers many merchants, gentry, and even nobles. This alarmed James, who had had his fill of the Presbyterian form of Puritanism in Scotland and believed it to be wholly out of step with monarchical government. "No bishop, no king," he said, meaning that if the church grew democratic to the extent of abolishing bishops, the next blow would be at the throne itself. When the Puritans stated their case to him, he grew angry and declared, "If this be all they have to say, I shall make them conform themselves, or I will harry them out of the land."

Neither side had a monopoly of justice; James's arguments had some point, but as the king was no statesman, his tactlessness only made a bad situation worse. Yet he did not actually "harry" many dissenters out of the country; the real Puritan emigration to New England took place in the reign of his son Charles I (1625–1649).

In addition to the Plymouth Pilgrims, various stray Englishmen now lived on the New England coast. These suddenly became a small minority, as the Puritan newcomers poured in. The Massachusetts Bay Company, which in practice was a corporation of Puritans interested in moving to America, took charge of the main migration. John Endicott founded Salem in 1628, and two years later over 900 colonists followed John Winthrop from England to found Boston. For years both Puritan and non-Puritan Englishmen came by thousands to the colony. Land around Boston was quickly taken up; settlers moved farther inland and expanded into New Hampshire and Connecticut. After some initial hardships, New England had by 1650 become a fairly thriving place, engaged in agriculture, fur trade, fishing, and shipbuilding.

The religious intolerance of the Puritan theocracy, with the clergy dominating so many phases of public and private life, has been much described and somewhat exaggerated.

When Roger Williams, a pastor whose views were too un-orthodox for the Massachusetts ministers, founded Rhode Island, he received some secret aid from John Winthrop. A few Quakers who ventured into Massachusetts were given a bad reception and some were even hanged, but from the evidence it is hard to escape the conclusion that they went there chiefly to stir up trouble. A Puritan would have an-swered charges of cruelty by saying that his community and church were so important that no chance could be taken of having them wrecked by outside mischief-makers.

Maryland

The founding of Maryland also had a religious motive. The Spaniards had not only warred against Elizabeth; they had employed English Catholics in plots to kill or over-throw her. Since then Catholics had been as much out of fa-vor in England as Protestant dissenters from the Established Church. George Calvert, First Baron Baltimore, was both a Catholic and a colonial promoter. Wishing to do something for his fellow churchmen in England and to increase his for-tune besides, he acquired from Charles I a grant of land on Chesapeake Bay north of Virginia. After his early death the grant descended to his more devoutly Catholic son Cecilius, the second Baron Baltimore. Cecilius and his brother Leonard started the Maryland colony in 1634. Like Virginia, this be-came a tobacco-raising settlement, with the proprietorship remaining in the Calvert family until the American Revolu-tion, except for a short interval in Cromwell's time. There was a mild Catholic flavor to Maryland, where some of the oldest families belonged to the Roman Church; but from the start most of the settlers were Protestant, and with religious feeling in England what it was, the Calverts would never have been able to introduce persecution, even if they had so desired.

The West Indies

While the English were establishing this line of mainland colonies, they also moved into the islands of the West Indies. Arriving at the same time as the French and the Dutch, they soon found themselves caught up in bitter international rivalry. Led at first by speculative proprietors, the English established themselves in several islands of the Lesser Antilles: St. Kitts, Barbados, Nevis, Antigua, and Montserrat. Later, when Cromwell ruled England, Spanish Jamaica was added by conquest. Settlers, including Puritans, poured into the English islands, at first in far greater numbers than they entered the mainland colonies, with the result that some of the islands became overpopulated, in spite of the high tropical death rate that carried off the earliest comers in waves. The introduction of Negro slaves had the effect of stabilizing agriculture on the new plantations, but brought with it an early stratification of West Indian society. Many surplus whites were crowded out by the land monopoly of the plantation owners and became aimless drifters who frequently furnished crews for the piratical buccaneers who plied the adjacent waters.

Cromwell and the West Indies

The quarrel between King James and parliament over religion, taxation, and fundamental principles of government continued at a sharper tempo in the reign of Charles I. In 1642 there began an English civil war that lasted seven years and ended with the victory of the parliamentarians, who emphasized the triumph by removing their former monarch's head. England now became a republic, but effective power soon slipped into the capable hands of Oliver Cromwell, Puritan commander of the parliamentary army. In 1653 Oliver took the title Lord Protector, or in plain words dictator, and governed the country alone until his death five years later. He is thought of by many today as a fanatic interested mainly in blue laws and religious persecution; he should be remembered as a great man of action and, above all, as an English imperialist. The Lord Protector disliked Spain, as most of his countrymen did. His principal grudge was not against Spain's religion but against the monopolistic trade policy that shut English commerce out of the Caribbean islands and mainland. Inspired by Thomas Gage, who had lived in the Spanish Indies as a priest but who had since turned Protestant, the Lord Protector planned a series of conquests to make England the paramount power in the Caribbean. As a beginning he intended to capture the city of Santo Domingo in the island of Haiti, and for this purpose sent a joint expedition in 1655 under Admiral William Penn and General Robert Venables. The attack was badly managed and was repulsed by the Spaniards. The two English leaders, not caring to face the formidable Protector empty handed, took the weakly defended island of Jamaica as a consolation prize, thereby adding a possession that would be of some importance later.

Cromwell, though disappointed, strove to make the best of Jamaica. To populate his new possession he seriously considered persuading the New Englanders to abandon their northern home and move to the tropical island. This idea never got past the planning stage, though it raises speculations as to how the Plymouth, Back Bay, and Connecticut

Puritans might have turned out had they elected to become Jamaica plantation magnates.

During Cromwell's regime the American colonies profited by another wave of migration from England. Just as Puritans had formerly left home because their faction was out of power, now many royalists, who for the time being were the underprivileged group, followed their example and migrated. Most of them went to the West Indies, but Virginia and Maryland, where Puritanism had little following, received some additional population.

The Restoration

After Cromwell's death, England and Scotland restored the Stuarts to the throne. The new king, Charles II (1660–1685), proved a poor substitute for the late Protector in foreign affairs, and for a secret cash consideration adopted the policy of truckling to the rich and powerful Louis XIV of France. Even so, the English empire continued to expand. Charles acquired Bombay as part of the dowry of a Portuguese princess whom he married in 1662, the Dutch settlements on the Hudson by conquest in 1664, and the colony of New Jersey by settlement a few years later.

Early in his reign a company of English speculators undertook to colonize Carolina, and in the far north another group, including the king's cousin Prince Rupert, founded the "Company of Adventurers of England trading into Hudson's Bay." The "adventurers" later set up fur-trading posts at a few strategic points along the bay from which, for nearly a century, the company was content to draw substantial profits from Indian fur trade without often venturing into the interior. In greatly altered and expanded form, the Hudson's Bay Company continues to exist and will celebrate its three-hundredth anniversary in 1970.

Pennsylvania

It was William Penn, Quaker son of the admiral who had conquered Jamaica for Oliver Cromwell, who founded Pennsylvania. With the large fortune that had come to him from his father, Penn inherited a claim for £16,000, which had been owed the admiral by the crown. As the acknowledged head of the Quaker sect, William Penn wished to follow Calvert's example and found an American colony for his people. Quakers were then highly unpopular in England; they were pacifists who would neither pay tithes nor serve in the army. They refused to take oaths, they dressed peculiarly, and some of them had rather freakish ways of emphasizing their religious convictions. Hence the English discrimination against them, while unjust, was understandable.

As payment for the debt, Penn accepted the proprietary grant of Pennsylvania, named not for himself but for his father the late admiral. He called his project a "holy experiment," and planned it with great enthusiasm. Before reaching Pennsylvania he sent a message to the Indians, saying "I have great Love and Regard towards you, and I desire to win and gain your Love and Friendship by a kind, Just and Peaceable Life." In 1682 he personally laid out the site of Philadelphia, the city of brotherly love, after concluding a series of treaties of peace and friendship with the Indians. Though he meant his colony to be a haven for persecuted English Quakers, he promised religious toleration to all settlers who might wish to come. Immigrants, many of them non-English, flocked rapidly to Pennsylvania; the promise of religious toleration was kept, and the prosperous colony remained a proprietary holding of the Penn family until the American Revolution.

Penn's original grant included the small area today known as Delaware, which the Duke of York had leased to him for ten thousand years. Differences between the Delaware and Pennsylvania settlers caused the former to break away, although the proprietor's family had some hold over them until 1776.

India

On the other side of the world, the English were beginning to build an empire in a totally different environment. Their East India Company had been started late in Elizabeth's reign as a loose organization in which each trading voyage to the East was an independent venture. Soon, however, the enterprise became a joint stock company, with permanent shareholders and continuity of policy. English traders first coveted the rich spice-growing East Indies, but found the Dutch too solidly entrenched there to be dislodged, and the company transferred its main activity to Hindustan. Several factories (trading posts) were acquired on the west coast of India, Surat being for a time the most important. Presently the factory of Madras was founded to provide a foothold on the eastern coast; and Charles II's marriage with the sister of a Portuguese ruler in 1662 was the occasion, as noted above, of the cession of the important city of Bombay in western India to Charles as part of the dowry.

Like its Dutch counterpart, the English corporation had been formed for trade with no intention of empire building. Not until the powerful Mogul Empire began to disintegrate in the years following 1707, leaving a vacuum of power in the vast, disunited, overpopulated peninsula, did the French and English companies begin to advance from trade to politics and from politics to war. Then for some years there was a struggle between the two for paramount power in India, a struggle which finally was settled by the Seven Years' War (1756–1763) in favor of the English.

Summary

As the eighteenth century closed, the English controlled an overseas empire centering in the Western Hemisphere. A great imperial prospect was also opening for their country in the East, but this was a matter for the somewhat distant future, since India was as yet only a source of profitable trade.

In the year 1700 England had a chain of North American possessions stretching from the isolated posts on Hudson Bay to the frontier of Georgia, which was still being claimed by Spain. Population figures for this mainland area are somewhat unreliable, but by 1700 the colonists must surely have numbered a quarter of a million. Large uninhabited and Indian tracts separated the settled areas, and few colonists lived far from the coast or inland rivers, since virtually all intercolonial communication was by water. Not for at least a generation would many of the gaps between settlements be filled or any important migration to the interior begin. The colonists had already become important producers and exporters of a long list of articles that varied according to geography and climate. Ships, lumber, furs, rum, tobacco, fish, and foodstuffs were sent abroad; and in spite of English mercantile laws domestic industry had begun to make its appearance.

The colonies were divided into three groups; New England, Middle Atlantic, and Southern; each with characteristics dictated mainly by geography but partly by the character of the settlers. New England with its town life, the Middle Colonies with their diversification of agriculture and occupation, the southern settlements with their emphasis on plantation agriculture and rural aristocracy, were each by 1700 displaying those qualities which would be their chief contributions to the culture of the United States. Slavery was legal and existed everywhere, but showed a tendency to concentrate in the south. Religion had a strong hold on all the colonies, yet nowhere was it so strong as in New England, where the influence of the Puritan theocrats as yet had scarcely waned. The Middle Colonies, still consisting mainly of New York and Pennsylvania, were the most cosmopolitan and contained the largest percentage of people of other than English stock.

The English mainland colonies had been acquired through military conquest, chartered companies, and individual proprietors. But with the conspicuous exceptions of Maryland and Pennsylvania, which remained proprietary until the Revolution, the trend was toward royal colonies, whose political relationships were with royal officers in London. In spite of this, however, self-governing institutions existed in all the mainland colonies, whether royal or proprietary, and the populations lived in part by laws of their own making.

In the West Indies the process had been somewhat similar, though limitations inherent in the geography and economy of the islands restricted the amount of self-government that could be enjoyed. Where the trading companies still existed, in India and in Hudson Bay, problems of government scarcely arose, since the companies were business concerns and did not care to expand their functions to include political administration.

The English colonies overseas, of whatever type or wherever found, were outposts to some extent of British interests, institutions, and even intellectual traditions. In many, it is true, the cultural heritage was slight and superficial, but in North America two colleges, Harvard and William and Mary, had been founded before the end of the century and another, Yale, was chartered immediately thereafter. The place of these institutions in the new rough-hewn world of their founders is simply described in a famous inscription which records:

After God had carried us safe to *New England* and wee had builded our houses, provided necessaries for our liveli-hood, rear'd convenient places for Gods worship, and setled the Civill Government: one of the next things we longed for, and looked after was to advance *Learning*, and perpetuate it to Posterity, dreading to leave an illiterate Ministery to the Churches, when our present Ministers shall lie in the dust.[1]

[1] Quoted from *New Englands First Fruits*, in Samuel Eliot Morison, *The Founding of Harvard College* (Cambridge, 1935), p. 3, and Appendix D.

Epilogue

AN EARLY eighteenth-century map compared with one made three centuries before would reveal at a glance how much man had learned about his earth. In 1400, a few years before Prince Henry's captains started sailing, the accepted picture of the world had not changed much from the one held by Seneca at the beginning of the Christian era. By 1700 the outlines of all the continents, except Australia, were known, and the seacoasts of the New World had been almost entirely explored. Circumnavigation of the globe, first accomplished by El Cano's *Victoria* in 1522, had grown so commonplace a century later as to call for no comment at all.

True, a great deal remained to be learned. The interior of Africa was mysterious, and many dark spots existed in giant Asia. The Antarctic continent, to the best of our knowledge, had never been seen by a human being and more needed to be known about Australasia. Vitus Bering would soon find the strait parting America from Asia, and even later Captain Cook would banish the concept of *Terra Australis*. Though these and other details of unfinished geographical business remained and though some would not be wholly cleared up by the mid-twentieth century, no future discoveries could possibly equal those already made. By 1700 the great unknown, the world of Prester Johns, Antilias, and Fountains of Youth, had vanished. Seneca might have reveled in the new knowledge, but he might also have regretted the passing of something that could not be recaptured; the belief in a wonderful world, populated by the more preposterous hopes and fears of the human mind.

Thus Europe had already gone a long way toward pre-empting the vast lands and populations made available by the white man's discoveries. Imperial powers, working amid distractions and at differing speeds, had persevered. The two original ones, Spain and Portugal, simply because they were the first, had built their empires in comparative leisure; but France, the Netherlands, and England had struggled to build theirs in an era of colonial rivalry and bitter international jealousy. During the first century of imperialism the Iberian nations had the outside world almost entirely to themselves. Then, around 1600, Frenchmen, Hollanders, and Englishmen surged forth to seize what they could of the prized Iberian possessions and to grasp at any new places that seemed worth the taking. Minor efforts at colonizing were made by Sweden, Scotland, and Denmark, but these were either brief or insignificant. And while western Europe reached beyond the ocean for empire, Russia stalked across Siberia to the Pacific and even temporarily beyond to Alaska. This Russian *drang nach osten* looms today as one of the decisive movements of history, but certainly it did not originate in the same background as the voyages of discovery and imperialism nor did it develop as a part of that movement.

Though the term "colonial empires" is loosely used here to designate all overseas dominions, conquest and colonization were not the same. Into such empty places as South Africa, Brazil, and North America, Europeans could freely move as settlers. In the Far East, Portuguese, Dutch, and English remained to the last a corporal's guard of palefaces, living and ruling amid the teeming native millions, whose essential way of life remained very little changed. In Spanish America both situations existed. There were the lonely pampas of Argentina offering opportunities to colonists, and there were also the rich and heavily populated regions of Peru and Mexico, ripe for the swords of the conquistadors.

Europe's far-flung dominions were the product of many different needs and motives. Individuals pushed to the farthest corners of the Old World and the New to seek gold, adventure, freedom from tyranny, or escape from justice. They went to spread the true faith, or sometimes to escape the toils of what others considered the true faith. Or else they went merely to trade, to farm free land, to grow rich, or to live in the hope of growing free and rich.

The rulers and governments that fostered and regulated all these efforts were motivated largely by a hope of profits, a hope conceived in mercantilistic theories and developed along mercantilistic lines. The different European powers formed their companies and built their empires in different ways, but across the gap of several hundred years it is the similarities in their methods that now stand out most clearly.

European governments felt always more interest in the quick profits promised by trade or treasure troves than in the more solid investment of colonies. For this same reason they liked to avoid the burden of colonization wherever possible. Taking a page from the feudal past, they often escaped the expense of colonies by throwing the responsibility of pioneering and development upon private individuals. The Portuguese called these entrepreneurs donataries, the Spaniards called them adelantados or encomenderos. To the French they were seigneurs, to the Dutch patroons, and to the English proprietors. These territorial lords at times stimulated colonization, yet often blocked it either by failing to understand the needs of the colonists or by insisting on terms that prospective colonists were unable to meet. One after another, with very few exceptions, these proprietarial dignitaries were removed by their governments and were replaced by varying combinations of local and royal administrators.

The early empires failed strikingly to live up to the economic hopes and visions that had presided over their founding. Although their impact upon the economy and culture of Europe was tremendous, the impact came in ways not foreseen or planned. The empires had all been started on the mercantile theory, in the expectation that they would enrich the mother countries by causing gold and silver to pour in. Gold and silver did of course enter Europe through Spain from Spanish America, but this could not make mercantilism a sound doctrine. Since real wealth consists of goods, and since silver and gold are but convenient measuring sticks for determining value, the arrival of all this bullion created no wealth but merely brought a rise in prices and a dislocation of European economy. Yet for centuries the governments of Europe stuck to mercantilism; each one trying, by colonial trade monopolies, to restrict commerce so as to pour cash into its own treasury and cut competitors out. The result was to keep trade from flourishing as it might have flourished and to force it into restricted, artificial channels. Europe, to be sure, was enormously richer by 1700 than in 1500, and the overseas world had contributed greatly to the increased prosperity. This, however, was in spite of mercantilism, not because of it. The true wealth consisted of the goods the outside world had sent to Europe, a flow that no mercantilistic regulations could altogether stop. Mercantilism had slowed the process of trade and wealth production; it could not stifle it entirely.

The colonists, in the meantime, failed to play passively the cut-and-dried role assigned to them. They were expected to buy the products of the mother country, to produce nothing that competed with those products, and to ship home raw stuffs priced much lower than the European goods they imported. The balance they were supposed to make up in cash. In so far as they were able, the colonists declined to do as they were told. When opportunity offered they bought goods, from whatever source, at the lowest price. Likewise, they sold when they could in the best market, wherever it might be. This uncontrollable tendency on the part of their colonial subjects added to the mercantilists' difficulties by making law enforcement very costly, since it required fleets of ships patrolling the seas, revenue cutters patrolling the shores, and many vigilant officials on land. In the contest between the law and the law evader, colonial public opinions tended to be with the evader, and rightly. The smuggler who brought cheap goods into a colony and the local merchant who dealt sub rosa with him were unintentionally greater fomenters of world prosperity than were the sage European statesmen who spent their time planning ways and means of enforcing the laws.

Before the end of the eighteenth century Europeans were realizing, even without Adam Smith, that mercantilism somehow did not pay. This realization came at about the time the old colonial empires were starting to disintegrate. The French empire all but vanished in the smoke of the Seven Years' War, and twenty years later the American Revolution deprived England of her best colonies. The Dutch empire dwindled under the impact of the French Revolution and the Napoleonic Wars; and by 1825 Spain and Portugal had lost most of their possessions through the revolutions in Latin America. Imperialism now reached its lowest ebb, as European statesmen doubted for a time that colonial empires were worth the having. Gladstone, the noted English Liberal, would cheerfully have disposed of Canada as late as the American Civil War. Not until near the end of the nineteenth century, as a product of the Industrial Revolution, was a new, vigorous concept of empire to seize the minds and inflame the imaginations of Europe's leading statesmen.

Although the old empires brought economic disappointment, it is not enough to assess their value in immediate monetary terms. More important than the profits the long-dead merchants failed to amass are the tremendous legacies of human alteration they left. Millions of Latin Americans today speak with the accents of the conquistadors, and the English language was first carried abroad by the sea dogs of the virgin queen. The United States sprang from roots struck in New World soil by chartered companies and proprietary grants. Alongside the failures and faults of early imperialism must be placed the story of millions converted to Christianity, the spread of European civilization to the ends of the earth, and the complete revision of European economy, scientific thought, and moral values. Neither the dark man who was conquered nor the white man who did the conquering survived the process unchanged. Seneca, the Roman philosopher who speculated so wisely on the secrets of the world, would have marveled at all this, but then, as he himself makes clear, he would have expected to be surprised.

Chronological Summary ~~~~~~~~~~

B.C.

6th century	Pythagorean philosophy; concept of a spherical earth.
c. 500	Hanno's voyage down west Africa, possibly to Sierra Leone.
4th century	Pytheas explores the British Isles. Alexander conquers to central Asia and past the Indus River.
3d century	Eratosthenes measures the earth's circumference.

A.D.

2d century	Ptolemy evolves the "Ptolemaic" concept of the universe: a round earth which is the center of creation.
7th century	Arab conquests following the death of Mohammed.
874	Iceland colonized by Norsemen.
985	Greenland settled by Erik the Red; almost simultaneous discovery of America by Bjarni Herjulfson.
1001–1016	Norse voyages to mainland America.
1096–1291	Crusades.
1165	Prester John letter circulates in Europe.
13th century	Mongol Empire in Asia; travels of Pian del Cárpine, Rubruk, and the Polos.

14th century Improvement of maps and nautical instruments; discovery of Madeiras and possibly the Azores and Senegal.

1415 Capture of Ceuta by Portugal; beginning of Prince Henry's discovery interests.

1434 Portuguese rounding of Cape Bojador.

1460 Death of Prince Henry; discoveries extended to Sierra Leone.

1482 Portuguese discovery of the Congo.

1488 Cape of Good Hope rounded by Dias.

1492 America discovered for Spain by Columbus.

1494 Treaty of Tordesillas; demarcation of Spanish-Portuguese influence.

1497 Discovery of North America for England by Cabot.

1499 Return of Vasco da Gama from India; beginning of Portuguese spice trade.

1512 Discovery of the Pacific by Abreu from Malacca.

1522 El Cano's *Victoria* completes circumnavigation of globe.

1535–1537 Exploration of St. Lawrence Basin for France by Cartier.

1541 Exploration of Amazon Basin for Spain by Orellana.

1553 Discovery of White Sea by Chancellor.

1580 Seizure of Portugal by Philip II. Completion of first English circumnavigation by Drake.

1588 Failure of Spanish Armada against England.

1595 First Dutch voyage to Far East.

1600 Formation of English East India Company.

1602 Formation of Dutch East India Company.

1607 Founding of Jamestown by Virginia Company.

1608 Founding of Quebec by Champlain.

1616 Discovery of Cape Horn by Schouten.

1620 Settlement of Plymouth by Pilgrims.

1621 Formation of Dutch West India Company.

1628 Beginnings of Massachusetts Bay Colony.

1630 Dutch West India Company invades Brazil in earnest.

1640 Portugal restored to independence.

1642–1643 Exploration of Tasmania and New Zealand by Tasman.

1654 Dutch expelled from Brazil.

1655 Conquest of Jamaica by England.

1662 Bombay acquired for England by royal marriage.

1664 Conquest of New Netherland by England.

1669–1687 Explorations in central North America by La Salle.

1682 Founding of Pennsylvania by William Penn.

1707 Breakup of Mogul Empire in India, opening the way for European conquest.

1713 Treaty of Utrecht; stabilization of old colonial empires for many years.

Suggestions for Further Reading

THE story of exploration in general is told by J. N. L. Baker, *A History of Geographical Discovery and Exploration* (London, 1948).

A good idea of the geographical attainments of the Greeks and Romans may be gained from M. Cary and E. A. Warmington, *The Ancient Explorers* (London, 1929), and from H. F. Tozer, *History of Ancient Geography* (Cambridge, Eng., various eds.).

The best one-volume survey of mediaeval geography with some account of discovery is George H. T. Kimble, *Geography in the Middle Ages* (London, 1938). A handy survey of travel from earliest times to the Portuguese rounding of Africa is Paul Herrmann, *Conquest by Man* (New York, 1954). Many books have been written on Norse discoveries; that by Gwyn Jones, *The Norse Atlantic Saga* (London, New York, Toronto, 1964), makes important original contributions. Lloyd A. Brown, *The Story of Maps* (Boston, 1949), is an interesting study of mediaeval maps and their gradual replacement by the newer-type portolans.

A true picture of what Marco Polo and contemporary European travelers found in the Orient is given by Leonardo Olschki, *Marco Polo's Asia* (Berkeley and Los Angeles, 1960). The likelihood that adventurous Europeans other than the Norsemen reached America in the Middle Ages is upheld by Frederick J. Pohl, *Atlantic Crossings before Columbus* (New York, 1961).

The peak period of European maritime discovery in the fifteenth and sixteenth centuries is described, though with different emphases, by Paul Herrmann, *The Great Age of Discovery* (New York, 1958), and by J. H. Parry, *The Age of Reconnaissance* (Cleveland and New York, 1963).

A fine survey of Portuguese explorations, with emphasis on the earlier voyages, is furnished by Edgar Prestage, *The Portuguese Pioneers* (London, 1934). Later Portuguese activities, including the problems of economics and empire building, are well handled by Kingsley G. Jayne, *Vasco da Gama and His Successors* (London, 1910). Portuguese imperialism until Brazilian independence is treated by C. R. Boxer, *Four Centuries of Portuguese Expansion, 1415–1825* (Johannesburg, 1961).

For Spanish exploration and colonization in America, the list of writings is very long. Much of the ground covered by William H. Prescott over a century ago has been more recently traversed by Roger Bigelow Merriman, *The Rise of the Spanish Empire in the Old World and the New* (4 vols., New York, 1918–1934). A shorter summary of Spanish conquests is furnished by F. A. Kirkpatrick, *The Spanish Conquistadores* (London, latest ed. 1963). The formation of Spanish institutions in America is described by C. H. Haring, *The Spanish Empire in America* (New York, 1947; paperback 1963). Two works by Herbert E. Bolton, *Outpost of Empire* (New York, 1931) and *Rim of Christendom* (New York, 1936), carry Spanish work into the southwest United States. Edward G. Bourne, *Spain in America* (New York, 1904; later reissued), is still one of the best.

On earlier French colonization, perhaps the best work available in English is Herbert I. Priestley, *France Overseas through the Old Regime* (2 vols., New York, 1930), which covers French activity throughout the world. For French pioneering in Canada there is, besides the older works of Francis Parkman, Bernard G. Hoffmann, *Cabot to Cartier: Sources for a Historical Ethnography of Northeastern North America, 1497–1550* (Toronto, 1961). The whole French North American episode is summarized very well by William B. Munro, *Crusaders of New France* (New Haven, 1918). G. B. Malleson, *History of the French in India* (Edinburgh, 1909), treats French activity in the Eastern Hemisphere.

Good works on Dutch activity and colonization have become more plentiful. Hendrik Willem Van Loon, *Golden Book of the Dutch Navigators* (New York, 1916), is chatty and inimitable in style. D. W. Davis, *A Primer of Dutch Seventeenth Century Overseas Trade* (The Hague, 1961), covers the world known to the

Dutch at that time. George Masselman, *The Cradle of Colonialism* (New Haven and London, 1963), concentrates on the home Netherlands and the building of the Indonesian empire. C. R. Boxer, *The Dutch in Brazil* (Oxford, 1957), covers in detail the material briefly presented on pp. 106–108 of this book. Since 1909 the Linschoten Society of the Netherlands has published original narratives of Dutch voyages and discoveries. These are all in Dutch, but many have been translated and published by the English Hakluyt Society.

Works on English voyages and colonization are so numerous as to defy classification. Many of the original narratives of English (and other) explorations, travels, and colonization attempts published by the Hakluyt Society since 1847 make excellent reading. The *Cambridge History of the British Empire* is factual, detailed, and sometimes dull, but can be recommended to any serious student of history. James A. Williamson, *The Cabot Voyages and Bristol Discovery under Henry VII* (Cambridge, Eng., Hakluyt Society, 1962), partly supersedes an earlier work of his on the Cabots. E. G. R. Taylor, *Tudor Geography, 1485–1583* (London, 1930), is excellent for the first part of England's overseas activity, as is James A. Williamson, *Age of Drake* (London, 1938). For the economic aspects of English colonization, Frederick C. Dietz, *An Economic History of England* (New York, 1942), is excellent. Daniel J. Boorstin, *The Americans: The Colonial Experiment* (New York, 1958; paperback, 1964), is a thought-provoking commentary on the English colonies in America.

In addition to the works above, the following biographies will be of interest: Germán Arciniegas, *Amerigo and the New World* (New York, 1955); Herbert E. Bolton, *Coronado on the Turquoise Trail* (Albuquerque, 1949); Henry H. Hart, *Venetian Adventurer: The Life and Times of Marco Polo* (Stanford, 1943) and *Sea Road to the Indies* [Vasco da Gama] (New York, 1950); Samuel E. Morison, *Admiral of the Ocean Sea* [Christopher Columbus] (2 vols., Boston, 1942); Charles McKew Parr, *Ferdinand Magellan, Circumnavigator* (New York, 1964); and Elaine Sanceau, *Henry the Navigator* (New York, 1947) and *The Perfect Prince* [John II] (Oporto, 1959).

Index